# Olde RECORDS Price Guide

## 1900 - 1947

### POPULAR AND CLASSICAL 78RPM'S

PETER A. SODERBERGH

Third Printing


Cover Illustration by Robert Sullivan
The Graphic Corporation
Des Moines, Iowa

Layout and Design by Marilyn Pardekooper
Edited by Elizabeth Fletcher



Published by

Wallace-Homestead Book Company
1912 Grand Avenue
Des Moines, Iowa 50309

To my retarded son, Peter — who was born free . . .

# Acknowledgments

I wish to convey my sincere gratitude to those persons who have expressed an interest in my work and given me both technical and moral support. I am obliged in particular to the following individuals who shared information and resources that I found helpful in the preparation of this manuscript: Don and Lou Donahue of The Olde Tyme Music Shoppe in Boonton, New Jersey; Harold Flakser, a knowledgeable man from my first hometown, Brooklyn; Roger A. Olson of Jamestown, New York, who contributed to my list of theme songs; N.E. Pierce of Jack's Record Cellar in San Francisco, a thoughtful observer who reminds us that a "fair price is one with which both parties are satisfied"; John Sicignano, a gentleman from Nutley, New Jersey, who gave freely of his opinions on reasonable pricing; and Frederick P. Williams of Philadelphia, the author of a detailed paper on collecting 78's.

I reserve a special niche for Harold Mire of Baton Rouge, a collector-dealer who assisted in the selection of the record labels pictorialized in this *Guide,* and Chuck Farrier who photographed the labels and album covers so expertly. I appreciate sincerely the sample evaluations of classical 78's sent me by Leon Kloppholz ("Mr. Records") of New Jersey; Rondo, Ltd. of Los Angeles; E. Spicer of Ontario; and George Collins of Canoga Park, California. Were it not for the clerical skills of Ms. Emily Aucoin you would be reading none of this, and I thank her, too. Of course, I accept full responsibility for the contents of this *Guide.*

# Contents

# Introduction

In this introductory section it is my intention to move from the general to the particular; i.e., *from* a commentary on the contemporary climate in which 78 rpm record collecting and pricing occur *to* a pronunciamento on the contents and function of this *Guide*. In between those extremities I will be as precise and as informative as possible. The essential purpose of this opening essay is to provide the reader with a modest framework within which you may *think* about 78 rpm records as properties to be sold, purchased, and/or retained (depending on your priviate motives) — but, in any case, cherished and respected. After all, 78's are vanishing icons of a receding era in our musical history and are worthy of dignified treatment. They do not always *look* like they deserve it, but they do.

In an earlier work, *78 RPM Records and Prices* (1977), I voiced the opinion that the current market for 78's was "brisk." Since the completion of that manuscript in 1976 I have eaten my words and revised my estimation several times over. I was much too conservative. The 78 rpm trade is not only brisk, it is bullish, lively, dynamic, exciting, and—at times—outrageous. How long this level of activity can be sustained is difficult to tell, but the crest has not yet been reached. History teaches us that boom times decrease in intensity eventually, so I am reasonably safe in predicting that the 78 rpm market will stabilize at a more rational plane within a year or three.

How did this outburst of renewed fascination with elderly disc records come about? There is no single answer. But I suspect a major contributing factor was the "Nostalgia Craze" that beset us early in the 1970s. Old records galloped back into the upper regions of our consciousness a few years ago when we grew nostalgic about the past, and they have been riding hard ever since. For reasons of establishing a proper backdrop to our approach to 78's, I invite you to reflect with me briefly on the ethos of this waning decade.

# Romanticism in the 1970s

The word "nostalgia" is derived from the Greek *nostos,* meaning "a return home." To remain with Webster for a moment, nostalgia is defined secondarily as "a longing for something far away or long ago or for former *happy* circumstances."

I italicize "happy" because nostalgia is very selective. Those who bathe in it generally dwell on (or yearn for) positive aspects of the past. After all, who wants to savor or relive in his reveries the cruelties, deprivations, and stupidities which characterize and afflict every generation? So, we repress the negative realities of the "good old days" and celebrate only what makes us feel good again. To quote Loudon Wainwright, "Nostalgia picks its way daintily through the ruins" of history.

The contemporary nostalgia binge is ten years old and shows no signs of waning (although it surely will fade in time). I date this near-melancholic condition from 1969-70. Absolute public confirmation of its presence came with the co-admission in *Time* (January 11, 1971) and *Life* (February 19, 1971) magazines that the nostalgia wave was "gathering momentum." As *Life* said of the new "sentimental craze for the past . . . Old is in, and we are happily awash in the sleek and gaudy period that stretched from the '20s through the '30s and into the '40s." Several years later Jack Kroll of *Newsweek* felt able to state that nostalgia had "become a semi-permanent part of the American psyche. . . ."

At first nostalgicism took the form of a revival of public curiosity about fairly broad representations of the past (art deco, vintage films, elderly musical comedies, comebacks by entertainers, etc.). By 1973 it had both intensified and crystallized into nostalgic specialties, which is usually the initial step toward becoming a big business. Suddenly a whole commercial enterprise rose up and the nostalgia trend lurched into high gear. Each stall in the gigantic warehouse of the American imagination featured a different nostalgic commodity — Depression glass, comic books, posters, campaign buttons, back-issue magazines, ration stamps, military regalia, and similar memorabilia from the first half of this century. And as our fascination with nostalgia deepened, the list of revered objects lengthened. Established dealers (coins, stamps, dolls, antiques) were swept along by the nostalgia tidal wave and became beneficiaries.

7

By 1976, stimulated perhaps by the retrospections of the Bicentennial year, everything—from fragments of junk to rare historical items—merged into a gargantuan pile of flea market goodies. Discrimination diminished and prices rose. The informality of yore was replaced gradually by a sort of commercial anxiety. (Irony of ironies, veteran peddlers of nostalgia began to speak nostalgically of the pre-Nostalgia era.) The nostalgia business has developed most of the attributes of a corporate endeavor: fierce competition, inflation, market fluctuations, publicity drives, house periodicals, and geographic apportionments. I should add, however, that (unlike the corporate milieu) the nostalgia world is not beholden to the ebb and flow of Wall Street fortunes. Indeed, even though prices may fall in the event of a national depression, the second-hand market will survive. Our yearning for the solvent past may even increase, then.

One more point before we move on to related issues. The nostalgia trend has received considerable attention, if not a boost, from the media at all levels. There is, of course, a prosperous Nostalgia Book Club. Newspapers mention the pattern frequently (cf. Tom Buckley, "Those Were the Days, the Good Old Ones," *New York Times,* April 14, 1974). Entire columns are devoted to the concept (cf. Thurlow Cannon's "Nostalgia Notes" in the Ogdensburg [New York] *Advance-News.)* Features in magazines refer to what we are doing to ourselves (cf. "The Collecting Craze: Yesterday's Junk, Tomorrow's Treasure" by Jim Salem in *America,* 1976). The inflight organ of Piedmont Airlines, *Pace,* hit passengers at 30,000 feet with Kay Shadoan's piece "Nostalgia Lives!" in January-February, 1976. Rebuttals and criticisms of what the Richmond (Va.) *Times-Dispatch* called our "obsession with back-pedaling into the past" have fallen on deaf ears. Evidently we like "the way we were" better than the way we are, and the media have found that tendency to be a source of "good copy."

Now we will tighten the focus somewhat and explore the residuals of the nostalgia fixation in arenas of concern to the collector/owner of 78 rpm records.

# Old Records As Commodities

Although the nostalgia movement has heightened public interest in *anything* old — the rose-colored spotlight shines primarily upon "collectibles" from the period 1930-60. The molten core of the volcano which throws up secondhand debris seems to draw energy from the movies, music, fashions, architecture, consumer goods, and other tailings produced between 1939 and 1945. Paraphernalia from the 1920s runs a tight second. Back beyond 1920 the market is less gaudy but the price tags are often very colorful. The thirties and forties are campy, close enough to be recalled firsthand by 43 million Americans, and are amplified by two unforgettable melodramas: the Great Depression and the last of the comprehensible, righteous world wars.

As you now realize, phonographs, cylinders, player pianos, sheet music, radios, jukeboxes, and 78's have been receiving an increasing amount of attention as the nostalgia epidemic spreads. (Nostalgia is a communicable disease. Everyone has a past.) There has always been a low-profile network of 78 rpm dealers and buffs — but for twenty-five years (1945-70) they talked and traded with each other only. As late as 1972, in his book *Collecting Nostalgia* (Castle Books; New Rochelle; New York), John Mebane devoted but a single paragraph to the old record market. He did advise us to secrete "scarce" discs until better days but he issued no alert that by mid-decade we would be enjoying an explosive renaissance in 78's. Very few anticipated it. Now that the mania is upon us it makes sense to examine the prevailing configurations.

The 78 rpm market appears to be divisible into four major groupings:

- **Popular:** meaning dance bands, vocalists, vocal combos, and small instrumental units who interpreted the fugitive "music of the year" for the listening public.

- **Classical:** strictly defined, incorporating symphonic orchestras, solo artists, and operatic companies who would not be caught dead wasting time on frivolous pop music.

- **Jazz-Blues:** being a highly intimate, universal musical language that transcends matters of time and space. Jazz-Blues may ease into the

9

Popular zone once in a while but Popular cannot return the favor, although it tries very hard.

- **Country-Western:** which is a musical form so distinctive that everyone recognizes it five seconds into any given record.

There is a substratum of 78's I might describe as the "Spoken Word." It includes speeches by heroes, politicians, and renown personages of the Cenozoic era of recordings — comedic monologues, vaudevillian duets, and similar non-orchestral efforts which are quaint but seldom inspiring. I suppose there exists a line of 78's one could call "Semiclassical." Therein reside singers (John McCormack, Nelson Eddy, Gladys Swarthout, James Melton, etc.) who were classically trained but defected now and then to the Popular category, and bi-musical orchestras such as Raymond Paige, the Boston "Pops," and Nathaniel Shilkret. As a final exercise in groove-splitting I note in passing the "Military" group, which was dominated by clones of John Philip Sousa (Pryor, Goldman, Victor Military, *et al*).

(To be technically proper I should footnote at this point that disc records did not stabilize at 78.26 rpm until 1925-26. Prior to the change from acoustical to electrical recording processes, disc records revolved at a multiplicity of speeds. For example, on a pre-World War I dust jacket in which a Columbia "Double-Disc" record was once protected, the statement "Columbia records are uniformly recorded at a speed of 80 revolutions per minute." appeared. In this *Guide* I take literary and generic license when I refer to all records listed as "78 rpm.")

# Record Owners and Dealers

People who own 78's fall generally into four categories:

(1) Private citizens who have small, personal (often "inherited") collections of the mixed-bag variety, and who are not impelled to worry very much about their holdings — until it occurs to them that they might have something "valuable."

(2) Serious collectors who are determined to improve the quality, and the size, of their stock over a period of time.

(3) Flea market entrepreneurs, antique shop proprietors, and the bazaar-garage sale regulars through whose nervous hands 78's will pass now and then, but who do not claim to be professional assayers of disc records.

(4) Professional dealers (who may be collectors also) who make a full- or part-time living from direct sales and auctions.

This *Guide* is directed for the most part at those among you who fit into the first three categories. There is probably very little I can tell (4) that he or she does not know already. Indeed, it is (4) who may take violent exception to the price levels I have set forth. I defer to his/her vast experience (without endorsing his/her susceptibility to overpricing).

People who fall into (1), (2), and (3) normally pose two questions early on: "Do I have any 78's that are worth a lot?" and, "How do I get in contact with a real dealer — to whom I may sell off my records, or from whom I may purchase discs I want?"

With regard to the first question, hopefully this *Guide* will proffer a satisfactory source of information. If you are interested in 78's of the Country-Western genre going back to the late 1920s then you would do well to consult Jerry Osborne's, *55 Years of Recorded Country/Western Music* (O'Sullivan, Woodside and Company; Phoenix; 1976). You will be pleased to discover that many of those old "hillbilly" 78's bring right smart prices on today's exchange. If popular and/or jazz-oriented records from the twenties to the late forties are what you wish to know about (assuming I have not covered your waterfront in this *Guide*) you might glance at Will Roy Hearne's, *Hollywood Premium Record Guide* (Hollywood, privately printed, 1948). Hearne recommended suitable prices for over 13,000 recordings, a labor of love he began in 1934 no less. You may wish also to have available Jerry Osborne and Bruce Hamilton, *A Guide to Record Collecting* (1979) which, in pages 1-12, gives you a tempting sample of prices on dance band 78's. This guide is published by O'Sullivan, Woodside and Company of Phoenix.

The second question, about dealers, can be discharged to your edification if you are willing to invest a little in two excellent fonts of information:

• Every year Kastlemusick, Inc. of Wilmington, Delaware publishes

11

its *Directory for Collectors of Recordings* in two volumes ($12.95).
You will find therein in excess of 2,100 listings of persons who can
dredge up nearly any record you may wish to buy, for a price.
Kastlemusick estimates that there may be as many as 16,000 dealers
in the nation today. Settle for one-eighth of them for openers and
procure the current edition of the *Directory*.

- In each of his three price guides Jerry Osborne signs off with a
  "Dealer's and Collector's Directory" section of substance in which
  he lists both foreign and domestic sources, grouped alphabetically by
  nations and states. Take a look at pp. 237-251 of Osborne's *Popular
  and Rock Records: 1948-1978* (O'Sullivan, Woodside and Company; Phoenix; 1978) and you will find some people who are still
  interested in 78's.

## The Importance of Record Condition

You will not be astonished to learn that the shape a 78 is in will dictate
how much it is worth. (Of course I speak now of commerce, not of
emotion. Each of us has a record or two which are priceless, even though
they are valueless in the marketplace.) Unfortunately, most 78's have
not been taken care of in a manner befitting a historical item deserving of
tender preservation. Often they are shuffled like screechy stacks of slate,
stored improperly, stained and fingerprinted, deprived of outer wrap-
pings, and otherwise maltreated. Some experts say that a battered 78 can
be restored by careful cosmetic practices (see Richard Gesner's series of
articles in *Kastlemusick Monthly Bulletin*, February through May,
1978), but I would keep my expectations under control.

There seems to be an ongoing consensus that we may rate the
condition of a record at from five to seven levels. Synthesizing the
various standards given us over the years by Will Hearne, Steve Propos,
Jerry Osborne, and Joseph Salerno I recommend you take another look
at your 78's from the following critical vantage points:

**Mint (M).** Perfect in every way. Free of defects in appearance,
magnificently devoid of surface noise. Probably never played.
Miraculously preserved from the ravages of time and mankind. A

gem in a costume jewelry world. Rare, delectable to behold, seldom seen by the human eye, priced accordingly. If you have a 78 of this caliber do not play it or touch it. Just sit down and stare at it in disbelief.

**Very Good (VG).** Sometimes superseded by "Near Mint" and "Excellent." Record shows little sign of wear physically. Some sheen remains. Has been played but transmits hardly any surface noise. No tics or blips. Equivalent to a cream puff used car driven to church once a week by that gentle old lady. Acceptable to collectors at near top price. Only purists with sonar ears would reject such a fine specimen.

**Good (G).** Getting a bit gray in the grooves and flaky at the edges. Still playable. Contents win the battle with surface noise during all but the last one-half inch. Victim of careless love. Luster gone but spirited in its attempt to reproduce sounds. Label starting to look grubby. Not incapable of bringing reasonable price if someone wants it badly enough. Hangs around flea markets hoping to be adopted by a nice family.

**Fair (F).** Borderline abject failure. Weatherbeaten. Mugged many times by thoughtless owners. Hiccups its way to fuzzy finish. Scratches and gouges mar sound. Surface noise suggests it was recorded in or near a broken steam pipe. Melody difficult to identify. Owner discouraged from playing record twice a year. Center hole creeping out toward edges of obliterated label. Preferred by people who collect rabid dogs, bent paper clips, and photos of Warren Harding.

**Poor (P).** Despicable remnant. Priced too high at five cents. Unplayable. Devours needles. Sends player arm back to you. Several hairline fractures. Impossible to discern contents. Grooves cut through to reverse side. Unworthy of decent burial. Bears absolutely no resemblance to whatever it was supposed to be. Useful only to break over head of person who tries to sell it to you.

It has been my experience that most Americans who have 78's are fortunate if their records are of the VG class, and are more likely to be the puzzled owners of G's and F's in great quantities. There are exceptions, naturally. It is not prudent to dismiss *every* record you have as worthless. That is why it is helpful to consult the appropriate price guide before you do anything rash. On the other hand, I regret to say, it is typical for the average citizen to assume his 78's have a higher value than the facts will support. Another, more painful reason, then, why it is judicious to see what the price guides have to report. It is more productive to know than to dream. Peace will come with the dawn.

One more word on this theme. Let me offer you a rule of thumb, the essence of which I borrow from Will Hearne's sober reflections on relative values. Let us presume your price guide tells you that the King Oliver record Aunt Agnes left you is indexed at $100. If your copy is in Mint or Near Mint condition then it is fair to assume it may bring you the full $100. If it is VG then it may be worth 75 percent of the top price; i.e., $75. G would reduce it to $25; F down to $15; and P (for such a rare item) perhaps to $3 or a bit less. Condition has a significant bearing on assessment. Develop a feel for it before you do anything dramatic with your 78's. And check with Aunt Agnes to see what else she has in stock.

## A Discographer's Manifesto

Before you plunge into the text there are a sextet of points I wish to make in the spirit of mutual understanding.

(1) I am neither a professional dealer nor a compulsive collector of 78's. I do have a modest cache of records from the period 1920-1957 but they are dear friends, not marketable properties. Simply speaking, I am a private citizen who has rummaged around in the facts, folklore, and fun of old records. I am knowledgeable, but fallible — just like you. If this *Guide* helps you assess your own collection then my essential goal will have been accomplished.

(2) In this *Guide* you will find 570 artists whose records you are likely to have (or stumble upon), rather than all artists who ever made records and every record they ever cut. I based my choices on years of wandering through places where used 78's were on display or for sale. I made notes on the sorts of records that turned up consistently, thinking that such

items might be found in the typical American's closet, attic, or garage. Thus, this *Guide* is intended to be more of a homeowner's manual than a record specialist's index. I leave the identification of exotica to other writers.

(3) You will notice that this *Guide* is interspersed with INTERMIS-SIONS. They are inserted for several reasons: (a) Everyone needs a break from the relentless format of a price guide; and (b) to suggest that there is much more to reflect upon than mere prices. A price guide is a non-book *de facto*. My interwoven mini-essays, perhaps, will lend a smidgin of intellectual substance to an otherwise surgical practice. I hope they will encourage you to learn more about the history of 78's and the artists who made them.

(4) I commence my listings of Popular 78's with 1917 (in general) because it was during that tense year (on February 26 to be exact) that the Original Dixieland Jazz Band first recorded for Victor. I realize there are earlier benchmarks to choose from — the dance mania of 1912-14; the formation of pioneer orchestras by Jim Europe, Art Hickman, Ted Lewis and others — but the advent of the ODJB I see as the opening curtain on an entirely new mode of thinking about music for the masses. It could well be viewed as the dawn of the pop record era. I end with 1947 because it was the last full year in which the 78 was dominant psychically. As for the Classical portion, Part Two, the selection of 1900 is rather arbitrary. It could just as well be 1901, 1903, or 1906. Choosing 1900 does permit me to catch most of the important developments on my way to 1941. I stop at 1941 because the Classical market was pretty well established by then, and many of the valued recordings we seek today were released prior to that year.

(5) Rightly or wrongly I have taken an anti-inflationary posture in my recommendations. The pricing spiral in 78's has been twisting upward inexorably since 1975 and I do not wish to support such a trend beyond reason. I expect the market will moderate soon. Meanwhile I maintain my conservative outlook without apologies, although I will aknowledge mistakes in judgment. You might be wise to compare my pricing levels with others before you make any irreversible decisions.

If I were to make a sixth point it would be this: When dealing in records, be they 78's or not, try to retain your sense of humor. Records are important, but they are not cosmic in their significance. Relax, enjoy yourself, maintain your equilibrium — and all good things (rare records, too) will come to you, in due time. Bon voyage.

# Decoding the Text
## Special Briefing for Readers

This *Guide* is divided into two major portions. Part One relates to "Popular" records of the vintage 1917-47. It might prove helpful to pinpoint several of its features before you plunge into the text.

**Presentation of Artists.** Without variation, artists included herein are presented in alpha order and appear in a format similar to this fictional (and totally implausible) sample:

**DOE, JOHN** and his orchestra

Stardust (Berigan, Dorsey)        (VIC 21234)     1/17/43   $5.00

Quite simply, this entry indicates that Doe's record *Stardust* (a) featured Bunny Berigan and Tommy Dorsey among the members who sat in on this particular session; (b) was cut on January 11, 1943 and released on the Victor label number 21234; and (c) may be valued at $5 on today's 78 rpm market. In numerous instances you will come across citations like this:

**DOE, JOHN**           NMP (.0-.50)

NMP stands for "Negligible Market Potential." Translated that means that John Doe records are valued at *less* than $1.50. NMP does *not* signify that Doe's discs are worthless and deserve to be consigned to the local dumpster. NMP merely suggests that if you own (or find) records by Doe's orchestra you are not operating in a lucrative area. Because Doe's prospects for being evaluated at more than $1.50 each in the foreseeable future are rather remote, he is NMP on that count as well. When some of Doe's records are worth more than $1.50, even though this will not alter his basic NMP rating, I list those exceptions and give individual prices. Now and then you notice a citation that looks like this:

**DOE, JOHN**           TIP

The symbol TIP says that an artist's works have "Trade Interest Potential," despite his previous NMP standing. Frankly, when I assign someone a TIP I am predicting an upswing in fortunes for his or her records. Sometimes record values rise when an artist dies; sometimes an artist's efforts do not strike the public's fancy on schedule; sometimes we wax sentimental and rediscover forgotten artists. Whatever the causative impulse, TIP means only that I anticipate the artist's records to increase in value within a few years. Thus, I urge you, preserve and/or purchase some of his or her key discs (if you care that much about such things). The essence of TIP is intuition. I have been wrong before.

## Operating Guidelines

Keep in mind as you proceed through Part One that: (a) my fundamental yardstick is a record that is at least VG in caliber; (b) if you are unable to find a given record it will mean (as a rule) that it cannot command more than $1.50 currently; although, if it belongs in a cluster of high-priced records I may have omitted it on purpose — assuming that you will infer its proper value from its surrounding contemporaries; (c) remember that records that sold a million copies or more in their day (see Joseph Murrells, *The Book of Golden Discs* (Barrie and Jenkins; London; 1978) are not likely to bring the level of prices rarer discs can elicit; and (d) an old 78 that has been reproduced on 33⅓ LPs since 1948 has suffered some loss in face value therefrom. Benny Goodman and Enrico Caruso have that much in common at least.

## Remarks on Part Two

The second, shorter section of this *Guide* is given over to "Classical" records, 1900-1940. Artists are alphabetized, embellishments are minimized. Listings are restricted to artists and orchestras whose records are placed at $2 or higher, and whose 78 rpm multi-disc albums are valued at $4 or more. No distinctions are made between one-sided and two-sided records.

In both Popular and Classical listings, but especially in the Popular, I cite only those records made in the U.S.A. I make no attempt at pricing discs cut overseas, although in many cases such records are more valuable than their domestic counterparts. I am not competent to assess the worth of records made by American artists at foreign studios, except in a very few instances.

Finally, you need to be provided with the abbreviations employed to indicate what labels are referred to in the text.

AEO (Aeolian)
AJX (Ajax)
APO (Apollo)
ARA (ARA)
ARC (American Rec. Co.)
ASH (Asch)
AUT (Autograph)
BAN (Banner)
BLB (Bluebird)
BLN (Blue Note)
BLU (Blue Disc)
BPT (Black Patti)
BRN (Brunswick)
BSW (Black Swan)
BWY (Broadway)
CAM (Cameo)
CAP (Capitol)
CAR (Cardinal)
CHA (Champion)
CMD (Commodore)
COL (Columbia)
COM (Comet)
CRN (Crown)
DEC (Decca)
DEL (DeLuxe)
DOM (Domino)
EDI (Edison)
EMR (Emerson)
GEN (Gennett)
HAR (Harmony)

HMV (His Master's Voice)
HRS (Hot Record Society)
KEY (Keynote)
MAJ (Majestic)
MAN (Manor)
MEL (Melotone)
MUS (Musicraft)
ODE (Odeon)
OKE (Okeh)
ORL (Oriole)
PAN (Panachord)
PAR (Paramount)
PAT (Pathe)
PER (Perfect)
PHN (Parlophone)
QRS (Quality Real Special)
REG (Regal)
RGS (Regis)
ROM (Romeo)
SAV (Savoy)
SIG (Signature)
SON (Sonora)
SWG (Swing)
VAR (Varsity)
VAY (Variety)
VEL (Velvetone)
VIC (Victor)
VOC (Vocalion)
ZON (Zonophone)

There you are. That is about all I can do for you by way of preparation. Now it is your turn. Come on in. The water is fine.

# PART ONE

# Popular Records (1917-1947)

# A

**AARONSON, IRVING** and his orchestra
  Generally NMP with these exceptions:

| | | | |
|---|---|---|---|
| Don't Wake Me Up | (EDI 51685) | 1/20/26 | $ 1.25 |
| He Ain't Done Right by Nell | (VIC 20034) | 4/27/26 | 1.25 |
| The Pump Song | (VIC 20083) | 5/15/26 | 1.25 |
| Hard-to-Get-Gertie | (VIC 20100) | 6/25/26 | 1.25 |
| I Never See Maggie Alone | (VIC 20473) | 1/07/27 | 1.25 |
| Sweetheart of All My Dreams (Shaw, Pastor) | (VIC 21834) | 12/21/28 | 2.00 |
| Outside (Shaw, Pastor) | (VIC 21888) | 2/06/29 | 2.00 |
| Moonlight on the Colorado (Shaw, Pastor) | (BRN 4883) | 8/22/30 | 2.00 |
| Lazy Bones (Krupa) | (VIC 25004) | 8/03/33 | 2.50 |
| Ah! But Is It Love? (Krupa) | (VOC 25005) | 8/03/33 | 2.50 |
| Snowball (Krupa) | (VOC 2535) | 9/06/33 | 2.50 |
| Thanks (Krupa) | (VOC 2536) | 9/06/33 | 2.50 |
| Goodnight, Little Girl of My Dreams (Krupa) | (VOC 2571) | 10/12/33 | 2.50 |
| Marching Along Together (Krupa) | (VOC 2570) | 10/12/33 | 2.50 |
| Commanderism (theme) | (COL 3043-D) | 4/18/35 | 1.50 |

**ALEXANDER, VAN**          NMP (.0-.25)

**ALL-STAR ORCHESTRA** (directed by Nathaniel Shilkret)

| | | | |
|---|---|---|---|
| Chloe (Miff Mole, J. Venuti) | (VIC 21149) | 12/13/27 | 1.50 |
| My Melancholy Baby (T. Dorsey) | (VIC 21212) | 1/03/28 | 1.50 |
| Oh, Baby! (G. Miller, B. Goodman) | (VIC 21423) | 3/21/28 | 2.50 |
| There's a Rainbow 'Round My Shoulder | (VIC 21667) | 8/09/28 | 3.00 |

**ALL-STAR TRIO**          NMP (.0-.25)

**AMBROSE, BERT\*** and his orchestra

| | | | |
|---|---|---|---|
| Singapore Sorrows (Ted Heath) | (HMVB-5464) | 4/02/28 | 3.50 |
| Sweet Sue | (HMVB-5508) | 6/27/28 | 3.50 |

| | | | |
|---|---|---|---|
| Embassy Stomp/Piccolino | (DEC 551) | 1/03/35 | $ 2.50 |
| Hor's d'Oeuvres (theme) | (DEC 500) | 1/04/35 | 3.00 |
| Dodging a Divorcee | (DEC 457) | 3/20/35 | 2.50 |
| B'wanga | (DEC 726) | 4/15/35 | 2.50 |
| Night Ride | (DEC 992) | 6/29/36 | 3.00 |
| Wood and Ivory | (DEC 972) | 8/12/36 | 2.50 |
| Champagne Cocktail/Tarantula | (DEC 1206) | 12/30/36 | 2.50 |
| Deep Henderson | (DEC 1526) | 8/08/37 | 2.00 |

*All records by Ambrose were recorded in England. The label numbers above are those on American Decca discs. Ted Heath was with Ambrose until summer, 1936.

## ANDREWS SISTERS
Generally NMP with these exceptions:

| | | | |
|---|---|---|---|
| Bei Mir Bist Du Schoen | (DEC 1562) | 11/24/37 | 3.00 |
| Hold Tight, Hold Tight | (DEC 2214) | 11/21/38 | 1.75 |
| Beer Barrel Polka | (DEC 2462) | 5/03/39 | 2.00 |
| Apple Blossom Time | (DEC 3622) | 11/14/40 | 3.00 |
| Boogie Woogie Bugle Boy | (DEC 3598) | 1/02/41 | 3.50 |
| Sonny Boy | (DEC 3871) | 5/29/41 | 2.50 |

## ARDEN-OHMAN ORCHESTRA     NMP (.0-.25)

## ARMSTRONG, LOUIS and his various groups

| | | | |
|---|---|---|---|
| My Heart | (OKE 8320) | 11/12/25 | 35.00 |
| Gut Bucket Blues | (OKE 8261) | 11/12/25 | 35.00 |
| Heebie Jeebies | (OKE 8300) | 2/26/26 | 35.00 |
| Oriental Strut | (OKE 8299) | 2/26/26 | 35.00 |
| Don't Forget to Mess Around | (OKE 8343) | 6/16/26 | 30.00 |
| Who's It? | (OKE 8357) | 6/16/26 | 30.00 |
| The King of the Zulus | (OKE 8396) | 6/23/26 | 30.00 |
| Sweet Little Papa | (OKE 8379) | 6/23/26 | 30.00 |
| Jazz Lips | (OKE 8346) | 11/16/26 | 30.00 |
| Big Butter and Egg Man | (OKE 8423) | 11/16/26 | 30.00 |
| You Made Me Love You | (OKE 8447) | 11/27/26 | 25.00 |
| Willie the Weeper | (OKE 8482) | 5/07/27 | 25.00 |
| Wild Man Blues | (OKE 8474) | 5/07/27 | 30.00 |

**Louis Armstrong**

Photograph courtesy RCA Victor

| | | | |
|---|---|---|---|
| Potato Head Blues | (OKE 8503) | 5/10/27 | $ 25.00 |
| Melancholy Blues | (OKE 8496) | 5/11/27 | 25.00 |
| Weary Blues | (OKE 8519) | 5/11/27 | 25.00 |
| Struttin' with Some Barbecue | (OKE 8566) | 12/09/27 | 25.00 |
| Got No Blues | (OKE 8551) | 12/09/27 | 25.00 |
| Savoy Blues | (OKE 8535) | 12/13/27 | 25.00 |
| West End Blues | (OKE 8597) | 6/28/28 | 10.00 |
| Sugar Foot Strut | (OKE 8609) | 6/28/28 | 10.00 |
| Squeeze Me | (OKE 8641) | 6/29/28 | 10.00 |
| Knee Drops | (OKE 8631) | 7/05/28 | 10.00 |
| Basin Street Blues | (OKE 8690) | 12/04/28 | 10.00 |
| Heah Me Talkin' to Ya? | (OKE 8649) | 12/12/28 | 10.00 |
| St. James Infirmary | (OKE 8657) | 12/12/28 | 10.00 |
| Knockin' a Jug | (OKE 8703) | 3/05/29 | 10.00 |
| I Can't Give You Anything<br>But Love | (OKE 8669) | 3/05/29 | 10.00 |
| Mahogany Hall Stomp | (OKE 8680) | 3/05/29 | 10.00 |
| That Rhythm Man | (OKE 8717) | 7/22/29 | 8.00 |
| Some of These Days | (OKE 8729) | 9/10/29 | 8.00 |
| When You're Smiling | (OKE 41298) | 9/11/29 | 8.00 |
| After You've Gone | (OKE 41350) | 11/26/29 | 5.00 |
| I Ain't Got Nobody | (OKE 8756) | 12/10/29 | 5.00 |
| A Song of the Islands | (OKE 41375) | 1/24/30 | 5.00 |
| Dear Old Southland | (OKE 41454) | 4/05/30 | 5.00 |
| I Can't Believe That ... | (OKE 41415) | 4/05/30 | 5.00 |
| Exactly Like You | (OKE 41423) | 5/04/30 | 5.00 |
| Tiger Rag | (OKE 8800) | 5/04/30 | 4.00 |
| I'm a Ding Dong Daddy ... | (OKE 41442) | 7/21/30 | 5.00 |
| Confessin' | (OKE 41448) | 8/19/30 | 5.00 |
| Body and Soul | (OKE 41468) | 10/09/30 | 5.00 |
| Memories of You | (OKE 41463) | 10/16/30 | 5.00 |
| You're Driving Me Crazy | (OKE 41478) | 12/23/30 | 5.00 |
| Just a Gigolo | (OKE 41486) | 3/09/31 | 4.00 |
| I Surrender Dear | (OKE 41497) | 4/20/31 | 4.00 |
| When It's Sleepy Time<br>Down South (theme) | (OKE 41504) | 4/20/31 | 8.00 |

(All OKE releases until April, 1932, same price range.)

| | | | |
|---|---|---|---|
| That's My Home | (VIC 24200) | 12/08/32 | $ 3.00 |
| Medley of Armstrong Hits (12″) | (VIC 36084) | 12/21/32 | 8.00 |
| High Society | (VIC 24232) | 1/26/33 | 8.00 |
| Basin Street Blues | (VIC 24351) | 1/27/33 | 3.00 |
| (All VIC releases through April, 1933, same price range.) | | | |
| You Are My Lucky Star | (DEC 580) | 10/03/35 | 2.00 |
| Old Man Mose | (DEC 622) | 11/21/35 | 2.50 |
| Putting All My Eggs in One Basket (Berigan) | (DEC 698) | 2/04/36 | 2.00 |
| Skeleton in the Closet (J. Dorsey Orch.) | (DEC 949) | 8/07/36 | 3.00 |
| Pennies from Heaven (Crosby, Langford) (12″) | (DEC 15027) | 8/17/36 | 4.00 |
| Shade of the Old Apple Tree (Mills Bros.) | (DEC 1495) | 6/29/37 | 1.75 |
| On the Sunny Side of the Street | (DEC 1560) | 11/15/37 | 1.75 |
| When the Saints Go Marching In | (DEC 2230) | 5/13/38 | 2.50 |
| Flat Foot Floogie (Mills Bros.) | (DEC 1876) | 6/10/38 | 1.75 |
| Ain't Misbehavin' | (DEC 2042) | 6/24/38 | 1.50 |
| Jeepers Creepers | (DEC 2267) | 1/18/39 | 1.50 |
| Rockin' Chair (Casa Loma) | (DEC 2395) | 2/20/39 | 1.75 |
| (All DEC releases until 1947 in $1.00-1.75 range.) | | | |

**ARNAZ, DESI**                                    NMP (.0-.50)

**ARNHEIM, GUS** and his orchestra
   Generally NMP except for:

| | | | |
|---|---|---|---|
| A Peach of a Pair (R. Columbo) | (VIC 22546) | 6/18/30 | 2.50 |
| It Must Be True (Bing Crosby) | (VIC 22561) | 10/29/30 | 10.00 |
| Them There Eyes (Crosby) | (VIC 22580) | 11/20/30 | 10.00 |
| I Surrender, Dear (Crosby) | (VIC 22618) | 1/19/31 | 10.00 |
| Thanks to You (Crosby) | (VIC 22700) | 3/02/31 | 10.00 |
| Ho Hum! (Crosby) | (VIC 22691) | 5/01/31 | 8.00 |
| There's Nothing Too Good . . . (E. Cantor) | (VIC 22851) | 9/23/31 | 3.00 |
| Evening (Buddy Clark) | (VIC 24061) | 7/02/32 | 7.50 |

| | | | |
|---|---|---|---|
| Exactly like You (S. Kenton) | (BRN 7904) | 5/19/37 | $ 3.00 |

## ASTAIRE, FRED — TIP

| | | | |
|---|---|---|---|
| Hang On to Me (with G. Gershwin) | (COL 3970) | 4/19/26 | 10.00 |
| Funny Face | (COL 5174) | 11/26/28 | 7.50 |
| High Hat | (COL 5173) | 11/29/28 | 7.50 |
| I Love Louisa | (VIC 22755) | 6/30/31 | 3.50 |
| Hoops (with Adele Astaire) | (VIC 22836) | 10/19/31 | 3.50 |
| Night and Day | (VIC 24193) | 11/22/32 | 3.00 |
| The Gold Diggers' Song | (VIC 24315) | 5/02/33 | 2.50 |
| Cheek to Cheek | (BRN 7486) | 6/26/35 | 4.00 |
| Top Hat, White Tie and Tails | (BRN 7487) | 6/27/35 | 4.00 |
| I'm Putting All My Eggs in One Basket | (BRN 7609) | 1/30/36 | 4.00 |
| Let Yourself Go | (BRN 7608) | 1/30/36 | 4.00 |
| Pick Yourself Up | (BRN 7717) | 7/26/36 | 4.00 |
| A Fine Romance | (BRN 7716) | 7/28/36 | 4.00 |
| They All Laughed | (BRN 7856) | 3/18/37 | 4.00 |
| Let's Call the Whole Thing Off | (BRN 7857) | 3/19/37 | 4.00 |
| Shall We Dance? | (BRN 7859) | 3/21/37 | 4.00 |
| A Foggy Day | (BRN 7982) | 10/17/37 | 4.00 |
| Nice Work If You Can Get It | (BRN 7983) | 10/19/37 | 4.00 |
| Change Partners | (BRN 8189) | 3/24/38 | 4.00 |
| Who Cares (with B. Goodman) | (COL 35517) | 5/09/40 | 5.00 |
| Love of My Life | (COL 35815) | 9/22/40 | 3.50 |
| I'll Capture Your Heart (with Bing Crosby) | (DEC 18427) | 5/27/42 | 4.00 |

## AUSTIN, GENE — NMP (.0-.50)

## AYRES, MITCHELL
Generally NMP with these borderline exceptions: 4/04/40

| | | | |
|---|---|---|---|
| Make-Believe Island | (BLB 10687) | 5/07/40 | 1.50 |
| Two Dreams Met | (BLB 10887) | 9/18/40 | 1.50 |
| This Is New | (BLB 11035) | 1/20/41 | 1.50 |

**Mitchell Ayres**          Photograph courtesy Alf Hildman, West Des Moines

# B

## BAILEY, MILDRED

| | | | |
|---|---|---|---|
| You Call It Madness (with Casa Loma) | (BRN 6184) | 9/15/31 | $ 5.00 |
| When It's Sleepy Time Down South (Casa Loma) | (BRN 6190) | 9/15/31 | 5.00 |
| Georgia on My Mind | (VIC 22891) | 11/24/31 | 5.00 |
| Dear Old Mother Dixie | (VIC 24137) | 3/01/32 | 4.00 |
| Rockin' Chair | (VIC 24117) | 8/18/32 | 4.00 |
| Harlem Lullaby (Dorsey Bros. Orch.) | (BRN 6558) | 4/08/33 | 5.00 |
| Lazy Bones (Dorsey Bros.) | (BRN 6587) | 6/06/33 | 5.00 |
| Someday Sweetheart | (VOC 3057) | 9/20/35 | 4.00 |
| Honeysuckle Rose | (DEC 18108) | 12/06/35 | 4.00 |
| For Sentimental Reasons | (VOC 3367) | 11/09/36 | 5.00 |
| More than You Know | (VOC 3378) | 11/09/36 | 5.00 |
| My Last Affair | (VOC 3449) | 1/19/37 | 4.00 |
| Where Are You? | (VOC 3456) | 1/19/37 | 4.00 |
| Never in a Million Years | (VOC 3508) | 3/23/37 | 3.50 |
| Thanks for the Memory | (VOC 3931) | 1/10/38 | 3.50 |
| Don't Be That Way | (VOC 4016) | 3/14/38 | 3.50 |
| Washboard Blues | (VOC 4139) | 5/09/38 | 3.50 |
| The Lonesome Road | (VOC 4474) | 5/09/38 | 3.50 |
| My Reverie | (VOC 4408) | 9/14/38 | 3.50 |
| Old Folks | (VOC 4432) | 9/14/38 | 3.50 |
| St. Louis Blues | (VOC 4801) | 9/29/38 | 3.50 |
| I Cried for You | (VOC 4619) | 1/18/39 | 3.50 |
| There'll Be Some Changes Made | (VOC 5268) | 3/16/39 | 3.50 |
| Gulf Coast Blues | (VOC 4800) | 3/16/39 | 3.50 |
| And the Angels Sing | (VOC 4815) | 4/24/39 | 3.50 |
| A Ghost of a Chance | (VOC 5086) | 6/27/39 | 3.00 |
| Sometimes I Feel like a Motherless Child | (VOC 5209) | 9/21/39 | 3.00 |
| Nobody Knows the Trouble I've Seen | (COL 35348) | 11/30/39 | 3.00 |
| Don't Take Your Love from Me | (COL 35921) | 1/25/40 | 3.00 |

| | | | |
|---|---|---|---|
| I'm Nobody's Baby | (COL 35626) | 4/02/40 | $ 3.00 |
| Blue | (COL 35589) | 5/15/40 | 3.00 |
| Everything Depends on You | (DEC 3888) | 6/13/41 | 2.50 |
| More Than You Know | (DEC 4267) | 2/12/42 | 2.50 |

**BAKER, KENNY**    NMP (.0-.20)

**BAKER, PHIL**    NMP (.0-.10)

**BAKER, WEE BONNIE** (see TUCKER, ORRIN)

**BALLEW, SMITH** and his orchestra
  Generally NMP but for the following:

| | | | |
|---|---|---|---|
| Nine Little Miles (Dorseys) | (COL 2350-D) | 12/02/30 | 5.00 |
| I Hate Myself | (COL 2406-D) | 2/03/31 | 3.50 |
| I'm Dancing with the Girl of<br>  My Dreams | (BAN 33060) | 5/11/34 | 4.00 |
| I've Got You on the Top of<br>  My List | (BAN 33078) | 5/11/34 | 4.00 |
| Forbidden Lips | (BAN 33065) | 5/11/34 | 4.00 |

**BARNET, CHARLIE** and his orchestra

| | | | |
|---|---|---|---|
| What Is Sweeter? | (BAN 32876) | 10/09/33 | 3.00 |
| I'm No Angel | (BAN 32875) | 10/09/33 | 3.00 |
| Emaline | (BAN 33033) | 3/23/34 | 3.00 |
| Butterfingers | (BAN 33015) | 3/29/34 | 3.00 |
| Baby, Take a Bow | (BAN 33029) | 3/29/34 | 3.00 |
| Growlin' | (BLB 5816) | 1/21/35 | 2.50 |
| Nagasaki | (BLB 5815) | 1/21/35 | 2.50 |
| Until the Real Thing Comes Along | (BLB 6487) | 8/03/36 | 2.50 |
| Make Believe Ballroom | (BLB 6504) | 8/03/36 | 3.00 |
| The Milkman's Matinee | (BLB 6593) | 9/24/36 | 2.50 |
| Shame on You | (VAR 627) | 8/05/37 | 2.50 |
| Surrealism | (VAR 633) | 8/13/37 | 2.50 |
| Knockin' at the Famous Door | (BLB 10131) | 1/20/39 | 2.50 |
| Jump Session | (BLB 10172) | 2/24/39 | 2.50 |
| Echoes of Harlem | (BLB 10210) | 4/05/39 | 2.50 |
| Ebony Rhapsody | (BLB 10341) | 6/26/39 | 2.50 |

| | | | |
|---|---|---|---|
| Cherokee (theme) | (BLB 10373) | 7/17/39 | $ 2.50 |
| The Duke's Idea | (BLB 10453) | 9/10/39 | 2.50 |
| Leapin' at the Lincoln | (BLB 10774) | 3/21/40 | 2.50 |
| Flying Home | (BLB 10794) | 5/08/40 | 2.50 |
| No Name Jive (2 pts.) | (BLB 10737) | 5/16/40 | 3.00 |
| Pompton Turnpike | (BLB 10825) | 7/19/40 | 2.50 |
| Night and Day | (BLB 10888) | 9/17/40 | 3.00 |
| Redskin Rhumba | (BLB 10944) | 10/14/40 | 2.50 |
| Good-for-Nothin' Joe | | | |
| (Lena Horne) | (BLB 11037) | 1/07/41 | 3.00 |
| You're My Thrill (Lena Horne) | (BLB 11141) | 1/07/41 | 3.00 |
| Haunted Town (Lena Horne) | (BLB 11093) | 1/23/41 | 3.00 |
| Spanish Kick | (BLB 11265) | 6/11/41 | 2.00 |
| Harlem Speaks | (BLB 11281) | 8/14/41 | 2.00 |
| Murder at Peyton Hall | (BLB 11292) | 8/14/41 | 2.00 |
| Things Ain't What They | | | |
| Used to Be | (DEC 18507) | 7/17/42 | 2.00 |
| Gulf Coast Blues | (DEC 18810) | 2/24/42 | 2.00 |
| Skyliner | (DEC 18659) | 8/03/44 | 2.50 |
| New Redskin Rhumba | (CAR 25001) | 8/12/46 | 1.75 |

**BARRON, BLUE** and his orchestra    NMP (.0-.50)

**BASIE, COUNT** and his orchestra

| | | | |
|---|---|---|---|
| Honeysuckle Rose | (DEC 1141) | 1/21/37 | 3.00 |
| One O'clock Jump (theme) | (DEC 1363) | 7/07/37 | 3.50 |
| Jumpin' at the Woodside | (DEC 2212) | 8/22/38 | 3.00 |
| Panassie Stomp | (DEC 2224) | 11/16/38 | 2.50 |
| Goin' to Chicago Blues | (OKE 6244) | 4/10/41 | 2.50 |
| Basie Boogie | (OKE 6330) | 7/02/41 | 2.50 |
| One O'clock Jump | (OKE 6634) | 1/21/42 | 3.00 |
| Bugle Blues | (COL 36709) | 7/24/42 | 2.00 |
| Royal Garden Blues | (COL 36710) | 7/24/42 | 2.00 |
| St. Louis Blues | (COL 36711) | 7/24/42 | 2.00 |
| Farewell Blues | (COL 36712) | 7/24/42 | 2.00 |
| Red Bank Boogie | (COL 36766) | 12/06/44 | 2.00 |
| One O'clock Boogie | (VIC 20-2262) | 3/13/47 | 2.50 |

**Blue Barron**　　　　　　　Photograph courtesy Alf Hildman, West Des Moines

**Russ Carlisle**        Photograph courtesy Alf Hildman, West Des Moines

**Bix Beiderbecke**
Photograph courtesy
RCA Victor

**Count Basie**                    Photograph courtesy Val Air Ballroom, West Des Moines

**BAUR, FRANKLIN**                                  NMP (.0-.10)

**BECHET, SIDNEY** and his various groups

| | | | |
|---|---|---|---|
| I Found a New Baby | (VIC 24150) | 9/15/32 | $ 4.00 |
| Maple Leaf Rag | (VIC 23360) | 9/15/32 | 4.00 |
| Jungle Drums | (VOC 4537) | 11/16/38 | 3.50 |
| Chant in the Night | (VOC 4575) | 11/16/38 | 3.50 |
| Indian Summer | (BLB 10623) | 2/05/40 | 3.00 |
| One O'clock Jump | (VIC 27204) | 2/05/40 | 3.00 |
| Lonesome Blues | (BLN 13) | 3/27/40 | 3.50 |
| Saturday Night Blues | (BLN 502) | 3/27/40 | 3.50 |
| Four or Five Times | (HRS 2001) | 3/28/40 | 4.00 |
| Sweet Lorraine | (HRS 2000) | 3/28/40 | 4.00 |
| That's a Plenty | (HRS 2002) | 4/06/40 | 4.00 |
| Shake It and Break It | (VIC 26640) | 6/04/40 | 2.50 |
| Old Man Blues | (VIC 26663) | 6/04/40 | 2.50 |
| Blues in Thirds | (VIC 27204) | 9/06/40 | 2.50 |
| Ain't Misbehavin' | (VIC 26746) | 9/06/40 | 2.50 |
| Save It, Pretty Mama | (VIC 27240) | 9/06/40 | 2.50 |
| Baby, Won't You Please Come Home? | (VIC 27386) | 1/08/41 | 2.50 |
| The Sheik of Araby | (VIC 27485) | 4/18/41 | 2.50 |
| Swing Parade | (VIC 27574) | 4/28/41 | 2.50 |
| When It's Sleepy Time Down South | (VIC 27447) | 4/28/41 | 2.50 |
| I'm Coming, Virginia | (VIC 27904) | 9/13/41 | 2.50 |
| Limehouse Blues | (VIC 27600) | 9/13/41 | 2.50 |
| The Mooche | (VIC 20-1510) | 10/14/41 | 2.50 |
| Rose Room | (VIC 27707) | 10/24/41 | 2.50 |
| Muskrat Ramble (12″) | (BLN 43) | 12/20/44 | 4.00 |
| Jazz Me Blues (12″) | (BLN 44) | 12/20/44 | 4.00 |
| Quincy Street Stomp | (BLN 517) | 2/12/46 | 3.50 |

**BEIDERBECKE, BIX** and his various groups

| | | | |
|---|---|---|---|
| Davenport Blues (T. Dorsey) | (GEN 5654) | 1/26/25 | 15.00 |
| Bixology (piano solo) | (OKE 40916) | 9/09/27 | 15.00 |

| | | | |
|---|---|---|---|
| At the Jazz Band Ball | (OKE 40923) | 10/05/27 | $ 5.00 |
| Royal Garden Blues | (OKE 8544)* | 10/05/27 | 4.00 |
| Sorry | (OKE 41001) | 10/25/27 | 4.00 |
| Somebody Stole My Gal | (OKE 41030) | 4/17/28 | 4.00 |
| Ol' Man River | (OKE 41088) | 7/07/28 | 4.00 |
| Rhythm King | (OKE 41173) | 9/21/28 | 4.00 |
| I Don't Mind Walkin' in the Rain | (VIC 23008)† | 9/08/30 | 6.00 |

*On OKE 8544 Beiderbecke's group is called the New Orleans Lucky Seven.

†On VIC 23008 T. Dorsey, J. Dorsey, and B. Goodman sat in.

**BENEKE, TEX**                NMP (.0-.75)

**BENSON ORCHESTRA**          NMP (.0-.50)

**BERIGAN, BUNNY** and his various groups

| | | | |
|---|---|---|---|
| It's Been So Long | (VOC 3179) | 2/24/36 | 4.00 |
| Let Yourself Go | (VOC 3178) | 2/24/36 | 4.00 |
| A Melody from the Sky (A. Shaw) | (VOC 3224) | 4/13/36 | 4.00 |
| I Can't Get Started (A. Shaw) | (VOC 3225) | 4/13/36 | 6.00 |
| If I Had My Way | (VOC 3254) | 6/09/36 | 4.00 |
| When I'm with You (E. Condon) | (VOC 3253) | 6/09/36 | 4.00 |
| That Foolish Feeling (E. Condon) | (BRN 7784) | 11/23/36 | 3.00 |
| Blue Lou | (BRN 7832) | 2/17/37 | 3.00 |
| Dixieland Shuffle | (BRN 7858) | 1/22/37 | 3.00 |
| Frankie and Johnnie (G. Auld) | (VIC 25616) | 6/25/37 | 2.50 |
| Mahogany Hall Stomp | (VIC 25622) | 6/25/37 | 2.50 |
| I Can't Get Started (12″) (theme) | (VIC 36208) | 8/07/37 | 6.00 |
| A Study in Brown (G. Auld) | (VIC 25653) | 8/18/37 | 2.50 |
| Black Bottom | (VIC 26138) | 12/23/37 | 2.50 |
| Russian Lullaby | (VIC 26001) | 12/23/37 | 2.50 |
| Livery Stable Blues (B. Rich) | (VIC 26068) | 9/13/38 | 2.50 |
| Sobbin' Blues (R. Conniff) | (VIC 26116) | 11/22/38 | 2.50 |
| Jelly Roll Blues | (VIC 26113) | 11/22/38 | 3.00 |
| In a Mist | (VIC 26123) | 11/30/38 | 3.00 |
| Davenport Blues | (VIC 26121) | 11/30/38 | 2.50 |
| Jazz Me Blues | (VIC 26244) | 3/15/39 | 2.50 |
| Night Song | (VIC 27258) | 11/28/39 | 2.50 |

**Bunny Berigan**                    Photograph courtesy RCA Victor

**BERNIE, BEN** and his orchestra
Generally NMP with these possible exceptions:

| | | | |
|---|---|---|---|
| My Buddy | (VOC 14494) | 12/22 | $ 3.00 |
| Swinging Down the Lane | (VOC 14537) | 2/23 | 3.00 |
| Who's Sorry Now? | (VOC 14555) | 3/23 | 3.00 |
| Henpecked Blues | (VOC 14585) | 5/23 | 3.00 |
| Driftwood | (VOC 14822) | 5/24 | 3.00 |
| Somebody Loves Me | (VOC 14584) | 7/24 | 3.00 |
| Tea for Two | (VOC 14901) | 10/24 | 3.00 |
| Mandy | (VOC 14939) | 12/11/24 | 3.00 |
| Oh! Lady, Be Good | (VOC 14955) | 12/18/24 | 3.00 |
| I'll See You in My Dreams | (VOC 14957) | 12/27/24 | 3.00 |
| Sweet Georgia Brown | (VOC 15002) | 3/19/25 | 3.00 |
| If You Knew Susie | (VOC 15037) | 5/19/25 | 3.00 |
| Yes Sir, That's My Baby | (VOC 15080) | 8/10/25 | 3.00 |
| Sleepy Time Gal | (BRN 2992) | 12/07/25 | 3.00 |
| Ain't She Sweet? | (BRN 3444) | 1/28/27 | 3.00 |
| Hindustan (D. Stabile) | (BRN 4042) | 7/28/28 | 3.00 |
| Au Revoir, Pleasant Dreams (theme) | (BRN 4943) | 11/14/30 | 5.00 |

**BESTOR, DON**          NMP (.0-.25)

**BLACK, TED** and his orchestra
Generally NMP but for these few sides:

| | | | |
|---|---|---|---|
| Makin' Time with You | (CHA 16174) | 11/17/30 | 3.00 |
| Maybe It's the Moon | (MEL 12209) | 5/31 | 3.00 |
| Little Girl | (MEL 12188) | 5/31 | 3.00 |

**BLAKE, EUBIE** and his orchestra

| | | | |
|---|---|---|---|
| Baltimore Buzz | (VIC 18791) | 7/15/21 | 10.00 |
| Sounds of Africa (piano solo) | (EMR 10434) | 7/21 | 12.00 |
| Sweet Lady (piano solo) | (EMR 10450) | 9/21 | 12.00 |
| Cutie | (EMR 10519) | 2/11/22 | 7.50 |
| Please Don't Talk about Me ... | (CRN 3090) | 3/31 | 5.00 |
| When Your Lover Has Gone | (CRN 3086) | 3/31 | 5.00 |
| It Looks like Love | (CRN 3105) | 3/31 | 5.00 |

**"The Ol' Maestro" Ben Bernie** Photograph courtesy Alf Hildman, West Des Moines

**Bailey Sisters featured with Ben Bernie**

Photograph courtesy Alf Hildman, West Des Moines

| | | | |
|---|---|---|---|
| Nobody's Sweetheart | (CRN 3130) | 4/31 | $ 5.00 |
| One More Time | (CRN 3111) | 4/31 | 5.00 |
| Thumpin' and Bumpin' | (VIC 22737) | 6/03/31 | 5.00 |
| Little Girl | (VIC 22735) | 6/03/31 | 5.00 |
| Sweet Georgia Brown | (CRN 3197) | 9/31 | 5.00 |
| River, Stay Away from My Door | (CRN 3193) | 9/31 | 5.00 |

**BLEYER, ARCHIE**      NMP (.0-.25)

**BLOCH, RAY**      NMP (.0-.50)

**BOSTIC, EARL**      NMP (.0-.50)

**BOSWELL SISTERS**
  Generally NMP except for the following:

| | | | |
|---|---|---|---|
| Heebie Jeebies | (OKE 41444) | 10/03/30 | 5.00 |
| Gee, But I'd Like to Make You Happy | (OKE 41470) | 10/03/30 | 2.00 |
| When I Take My Sugar to Tea (Dorsey Bros.) | (BRN 6083) | 3/19/31 | 2.50 |
| Roll On, Mississippi, Roll On (Dorsey Bros.) | (BRN 6109) | 4/23/31 | 2.50 |
| I Found a Million Dollar Baby (Victor Young) | (BRN 6128) | 5/25/31 | 2.00 |
| It's the Girl (Dorsey Bros.) | (BRN 6151) | 7/08/31 | 2.50 |
| Heebies Jeebies (Dorsey Bros.) | (BRN 6173) | 8/27/31 | 2.50 |
| There'll Be Some Changes Made (Dorsey Bros.) | (BRN 6291) | 3/21/32 | 3.00 |
| It Don't Mean a Thing (Dorsey Bros.) | (BRN 6442) | 11/22/32 | 3.00 |
| Mood Indigo (Dorsey Bros.) | (BRN 6470) | 1/09/33 | 2.50 |
| Shuffle Off to Buffalo (Dorsey Bros.) | (BRN 6545) | 4/11/33 | 2.50 |
| The Object of My Affection (J. Grier) | (BRN 7348) | 12/10/34 | 2.00 |

## BOSWELL, CONNEE
Generally NMP but for:

| | | | |
|---|---|---|---|
| I'm Gonna Cry | (VIC 19639) | 3/22/25 | $ 4.00 |
| Washboard Blues (Casa Loma) | (BRN 20108) | 3/16/32 | 3.00 |
| I'll Never Say "Never Again" | | | |
| Again (Ambrose) | (BRN 02046) | 7/19/35 | 3.00 |
| Basin Street Blues (Bing Crosby) | (DEC 1483) | 9/25/37 | 4.00 |
| Ah! So Pure (Bob Crosby) | (DEC 1600) | 11/13/37 | 3.00 |
| Alexander's Ragtime Band | | | |
| (Crosby, Cantor) | (DEC 1887) | 1/26/38 | 6.00 |
| An Apple for the Teacher | | | |
| (Bing Crosby) | (DEC 2640) | 6/22/39 | 3.00 |
| Between 18th and 19th . . . | | | |
| (Bing Crosby) | (DEC 2948) | 12/15/39 | 3.00 |
| Yes, Indeed! (Bing Crosby) | (DEC 3689) | 12/13/40 | 3.00 |

## BRADLEY, WILL and his orchestra
Generall NMP but for these:

| | | | |
|---|---|---|---|
| Celery Stalks at Midnight/ | | | |
| Down the Road Apiece | (COL 35707) | 1/17/40 | 2.50 |
| Beat Me, Daddy, Eight to the | | | |
| Bar (2 pts.) | (COL 35530) | 5/21/40 | 3.00 |
| Scrub Me, Mama, with a | | | |
| Boogie Beat | (COL 35743) | 9/18/40 | 2.00 |
| Tea for Two | | | |
| (Ray McKinley Quartet) | (COL 36101) | 1/21/41 | 3.00 |
| Hall of the Mountain King | (COL 36286) | 5/12/41 | 2.00 |
| Fry Me, Cookie, with a | | | |
| Can of Lard | (COL 36719) | 10/16/41 | 1.75 |

## BRADSHAW, TINY                NMP (.0-1.00)

## BRANDWYNNE, NAT and his orchestra
Generally NMP with these exceptions:

| | | | |
|---|---|---|---|
| The Glory of Love (Buddy Clark) | (BRN 7660) | 4/13/36 | 2.00 |
| It's You I'm Talking About | | | |
| (B. Clark) | (BRN 7655) | 4/13/36 | 2.00 |

**Henry Busse**     Photograph courtesy Alf Hildman, West Des Moines

| | | | |
|---|---|---|---|
| These Foolish Things (B. Clark) | (BRN 7676) | 5/25/36 | $ 2.00 |
| Long Ago and Far Away (B. Clark) | (BRN 7678) | 5/25/36 | 2.00 |
| Until Today (B. Clark) | (BRN 7712) | 7/23/36 | 2.00 |
| Bye, Bye, Baby (B. Clark) | (BRN 7714) | 7/23/36 | 2.00 |

**BREESE, LOU**                      NMP (.0-.25)

**BROWN, LES**

Generally NMP with these few exceptions:

| | | | |
|---|---|---|---|
| Swing for Sale | (DEC 991) | 10/15/36 | 5.00 |
| Boogie Woogie | (BLB 7858) | 9/30/38 | 4.00 |
| Perisphere Shuffle | (BLB 10314) | 6/01/39 | 4.00 |
| Let's Be Buddies (Doris Day) | (OKE 5937) | 11/29/40 | 4.50 |
| Bizet Has His Day | (COL 36688) | 9/17/41 | 3.00 |
| Mexican Hat Dance | (OKE 6696) | 9/17/41 | 3.00 |
| Sunday | (COL 36724) | 7/20/42 | 2.50 |

**BRYANT, WILLIE** and his orchestra

| | | | |
|---|---|---|---|
| Throwin' Stones at the Sun | (VIC 24847) | 1/04/35 | 2.50 |
| A Viper's Moan | (VIC 24858) | 1/04/35 | 2.50 |
| Rigamarole | (VIC 25038) | 5/08/35 | 2.50 |
| 'Long about Midnight | (VIC 25045) | 5/08/35 | 2.50 |
| Voice of Old Man River | (VIC 25129) | 8/01/35 | 2.50 |
| Liza | (VIC 25160) | 8/01/35 | 2.50 |
| All My Life | (BLB 6361) | 4/09/36 | 2.00 |
| Ride, Red, Ride | (BLB 6374) | 4/09/36 | 2.00 |
| Moonrise on the Lowlands | (BLB 6362) | 4/09/36 | 2.00 |
| I Like Bananas | (BLB 6436) | 6/03/36 | 2.00 |
| Cross Patch | (BLB 6435) | 6/03/36 | 2.00 |

**BURKE, SONNY**                   NMP (.0-.50)

**BURR, HENRY**                     NMP (.0-.20)

**BUSSE, HENRY**                   NMP (.0-1.00)

**BUTTERFIELD, BILLY**           NMP (.0-1.00)

**BYRNE, BOBBY**                   NMP (.0-.50)

# INTERMISSION 1

## *Record Owners' Reading List*

You may recall from my Introduction to this *Guide* that I had hopes that it would prove to be something more than an exhaustive itemization of prices. My estimation of you, the reader, is quite high, actually. I really do believe that when given the opportunity to expand your knowledge of a subject, you will react in a positive, sophisticated manner. People who own or actively collect 78's are usually mature enough and affectionate enough to want to know more about records than their "going price." Therefore, I feel quite comfortable urging you to read the best in record-related literature. A little scholarship will go a long way toward making you a well-rounded record owner. You will be better able to speak with authority about old records and the milieu in which they were produced, and your appreciation for their individual and collective importance will be greatly enhanced. For your convenience I simply cite what I consider to be major reading categories and mention a few works within each. Naturally there are literary delights too numerous to include here, but these constitute a decent beginning. Remember, the focus is on the period 1900-1947, and most of the books listed were published in the 1970s.

**Periodicals.** *American Collector, Antiques Journal, Billboard, Down Beat, Hobbies, Kastlemusick Monthly Bulletin, The Record Finder*, annual anniversary edition of *Variety*. Only *Kastlemusick* and *The Record Finder* address themselves regularly to the vintage record business.

**Biographic Studies.** In the 1970s a fairly substantial output of books on personalities who contributed to the pop music of the 1920-50 period was evident. To name some of the artists whose lives were chronicled: Bix Beiderbecke, Cab Calloway, Duke Ellington, Billie Holiday, Guy Lombardo, Ozzie Nelson, and Fats Waller. Special works of this genre were: Herb Sanford, *Tommy and Jimmy: The Dorsey Years* (Arlington House; New Rochelle, New York, 1972); and George Simon, *Glenn*

*Miller and His Orchestra* (Arlington House; New Rochelle, New York, 1974), goldmines that contain many nuggets of insight into the big band era.

**General Works:** A class of up-tempo books which lend perspective to the current fascination with the past, notably among them: Jim Haskin's, *The Cotton Club* (Random House; New York, 1977); Albert Murray, *Stomping the Blues* (McGraw-Hill; New York, 1976); and Tony Palmer, *All You Need Is Love: The Story of Popular Music* (Penguin Books, New York, 1977).

**Reference Material:** There are a number of "encyclopedias" which cover various aspects of the jazz-blues-pop world but there is only one that can satisfy the curiosity of the pre-1950 record enthusiast: Roger D. Kinkle's, *The Complete Encyclopedia of Popular Music and Jazz: 1900-1950* (Arlington House; New Rochelle, New York; 1974), in four indispensable volumes.

**Discographies:** Once upon a time there was only Charles Delauney and his *New Hot Discography* (Criterion; New York, 1948), but in recent years this painstaking field has been dominated by Brian Rust, a reliable, thorough researcher who spares nothing in his wish to be accurate. If you want to know who recorded what, when — then you should consult Rust's: *The Complete Entertainment Discography* (Arlington House; New Rochelle, New York, 1973); *The American Dance Band Discography, 1917-1942* (Arlington House; New Rochelle, New York, 1975), two volumes; and *Jazz Records, 1917-1942* (Arlington House; New Rochelle, New York, 1978), two volumes. Not to be overshadowed are several other efforts of this type: D. Russell Connor and Warren H. Hicks, *BG (Benny Goodman) on the Record* (Arlington House; New Rochelle, New York, 1975) and John Flower's, *Moonlight Serenade: A Bio-Discography of the Glenn Miller Civilian Band* (Arlington House; New Rochelle, New York, 1972).

**Special Studies:** J. Krivine, *Juke Box Saturday Night* (Chartwell Books; Secaucus, New Jersey, 1977) is a delicious visual revisitation to the realm of coin-operated phonograph machines. If you ever wondered how many times pop musicians appeared in the cinema the David

Meeker's, *Jazz in the Movies* (Arlington House; New Rochelle, New York, 1977) is a filmographic listing you will enjoy. You will also find fascinating Brian Rust's *The American Record Label Book* (Arlington House; New Rochelle, New York, 1978), which takes you on a colorful tour of all those labels you admired from 1895 to 1942.

**Historical Works:** For a few dollars you can start your record-lover's library with two readable, illuminating books, both of which were revised in time to commemorate the centennial of the phonograph: Roland Gelatt, *The Fabulous Phonograph: 1877-1977* (Collier Books; New York, 1977) and Oliver Read and Walter L. Welch, *From Tin Foil to Stereo* (H.W. Sams; Indianapolis, 1976). If you have these you do not need much more history.

**Books about the Dance Bands:** This is a very exciting, prolific grouping of works that combine fulsome narratives with marvelous pictorials. We started the decade off with Gene Fernett's, *Swing Out: Great Negro Dance Bands* (Pendell Publishing Company; Detroit, 1970) and then came: Albert McCarthy, *The Dance Band Era* (Arlington House; New Rochelle, New York, 1974) and *Big Band Jazz* (Berkeley Publishing Corporation; New York, 1977); Brian Rust, *The Dance Bands* (Arlington House; New Rochelle, New York, 1974); George Simon, *The Big Bands* (Collier; New York, 1974) and *Simon Says: The Sights and Sounds of the Swing Era* (Arlington House; New Rochelle, New York, 1971); Leo Walker, *The Wonderful Era of the Great Dance Bands* (Doubleday; New York, 1972) and *Big Band Almanac* (Ward Ritchie Press; Pasadena, 1978).

**Privately Printed Materials:** There is much to be learned from books and pamphlets published by authors who cannot (or will not) have their research handled by the major companies. There are too many to note in this particular space but I have chosen a representative quartet of diverse intent as examples of this intriguing category: Charles Hager, *When Was That Old Record Made?* (Dallas, 1973); E.R. Fenimore Johnson, *His Master's Voice Was Eldridge P. Johnson* (Milford, Delaware, 1974); Richard N. Mellor, *Spotlights of Fame* (E. Natick, Massachusetts; 1953), a still-available compendium of show biz theme songs; and

Frederick P. Williams, ''Ideas on Beginning a 78's Record Collection'' (Philadelphia, 1973).

**Classical Records:** See Julian Morton Moses, *Collectors' Guide to American Recordings: 1895-1925* (Dover Publications; New York, 1977), the latest in a series of revisions of a seminal work undertaken originally by Moses in 1936.

# C

**CALLOWAY, CAB** and his orchestra

| | | | |
|---|---|---|---|
| St. Louis Blues | (BRN 4936) | 7/24/30 | $ 4.00 |
| Sweet Jennie Lee | (BAN 0847) | 10/14/30 | 4.50 |
| Some of These Days | (BRN 6020) | 12/23/30 | 4.00 |
| St. James' Infirmary | (BRN 6105) | 12/23/30 | 4.50 |
| Dixie Vagabond | (BAN 32116) | 3/03/31 | 4.00 |
| Minnie the Moocher (theme) | (BRN 6074) | 3/03/31 | 5.00 |
| Mood Indigo | (BAN 32152) | 3/09/31 | 4.50 |
| Creole Love Song | (BAN 32185) | 5/06/31 | 4.00 |
| The Levee Low Down | (BAN 32221) | 5/06/31 | 4.00 |
| Black Rhythm | (BRN 6141) | 6/11/31 | 4.00 |
| My Honey's Lovin' Arms | (BAN 32227) | 6/17/31 | 4.00 |
| Basin Street Blues | (BAN 32237) | 7/09/31 | 4.00 |
| Bugle Call Rag | (BRN 6196) | 9/23/31 | 4.00 |
| Stardust | (BAN 32295) | 10/12/31 | 4.50 |
| Kickin' the Gong Around | (BRN 6209) | 10/21/31 | 4.00 |
| Cabin in the Cotton | (BRN 6272) | 2/29/32 | 4.00 |
| Minnie the Moocher's Wedding Day | (BRN 6321) | 4/20/32 | 4.00 |
| Dinah | (BAN 32483) | 6/07/32 | 4.50 |
| You Gotta Ho-De-Ho | (BAN 32945) | 6/09/32 | 4.00 |
| Evenin' | (VIC 24414) | 9/18/33 | 3.50 |
| Harlem Camp Meeting | (VIC 24494) | 11/02/33 | 3.50 |
| Jitterbug | (VIC 24592) | 1/22/34 | 3.50 |
| Miss Otis Regrets | (BRN 7504) | 7/02/35 | 4.00 |
| Jonah Joins the Cab | (OKE 6109) | 3/05/41 | 2.50 |
| St. James' Infirmary | (OKE 6391) | 7/03/41 | 3.00 |
| Virginia, Georgia and Caroline | (OKE 6574) | 12/24/41 | 2.50 |
| Minnie the Moocher | (OKE 6634) | 2/02/42 | 2.50 |
| Hi-De-Ho Man | (COL 37312) | 2/03/47 | 2.50 |

**CARLE, FRANKIE** NMP (.0-1.25)

**CARMICHAEL, HOAGY\*** and his various groups

| | | | |
|---|---|---|---|
| Stardust | (GEN 6311) | 10/31/27 | 30.00 |
| Walkin' the Dog | (GEN 6474) | 5/02/28 | 10.00 |

**Cab Calloway**                    Photograph courtesy Alf Hildman, West Des Moines

| | | | |
|---|---|---|---|
| Rockin' Chair (T. Dorsey, B.G.) | (VIC 38139) | 5/21/30 | $ 7.50 |
| Georgia on My Mind | (VIC 23013) | 9/15/30 | 7.50 |
| Lazy River | (VIC 23034) | 11/20/30 | 7.50 |
| Lazy Bones (piano solo) | (VIC 24402) | 9/13/33 | 5.00 |
| Stardust (piano solo) | (VIC 24484) | 12/06/33 | 7.50 |
| Judy (the Dorseys) | (VIC 24627) | 3/09/34 | 5.00 |
| Hong Kong Blues (Spike Jones) | (BRN 8255) | 10/14/38 | 4.00 |
| Stardust (theme) | (DEC 18395) | 5/11/42 | 2.00 |

*Among those sitting in on VIC 23013, 23034 were the Dorseys, Bix Beiderbecke, Jack Teagarden, Eddie Lang, and Joe Venuti.

## CARTER, BENNY* and his various groups

| | | | |
|---|---|---|---|
| Swing It | (COL CB-628) | 3/14/33 | 4.00 |
| Synthetic Love | (COL CB-636) | 3/14/33 | 4.00 |
| Devil's Holiday | (COL 2898D) | 10/16/33 | 4.00 |
| Blue Lou | (OKE 41567) | 10/16/33 | 4.00 |
| Shoot the Works | (VOC 2898) | 12/13/34 | 3.50 |
| Everybody Shuffle | (VOC 2870) | 12/13/34 | 3.50 |
| Plymouth Rock | (VOC 4984) | 6/29/39 | 3.50 |
| Savoy Stampede | (VOC 5112) | 6/29/39 | 3.50 |
| Shufflebug Shuffle | (VOC 5508) | 11/01/39 | 3.50 |
| Slow Freight | (VOC 5399) | 1/30/40 | 3.50 |
| Beale St. Blues | (OKE 6001) | 10/15/40 | 3.50 |
| All of Me | (BLB 10962) | 11/19/40 | 3.00 |
| Back Bay Boogie | (BLB 11341) | 10/16/41 | 3.00 |
| Poinciana | (CAP 144) | 10/25/43 | 3.50 |
| I Surrender Dear/Malibu (4/9/45) | (CAP 200) | 5/21/44 | 3.50 |
| Stormy Weather | (CAP 283) | 4/02/45 | 2.75 |

*Carter cut many records overseas (London, Paris, The Hague, etc.) between 1936-38. By and large these sides are excellent musically and held in high financial esteem by collectors. None of them are listed above.

## CASA LOMA ORCHESTRA and GLEN GRAY*

| | | | |
|---|---|---|---|
| Love Is a Dreamer | (OKE 41329) | 10/29/29 | 7.50 |
| Happy Days Are Here Again | (OKE 41339) | 10/29/29 | 4.00 |

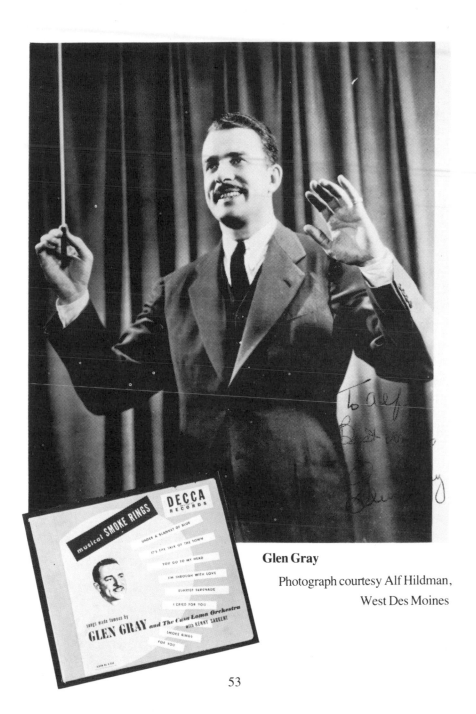

**Glen Gray**

Photograph courtesy Alf Hildman,
West Des Moines

53

| | | | |
|---|---|---|---|
| China Girl | (OKE 41403) | 2/11/30 | $ 7.50 |
| Casa Loma Stomp | (OKE 41492) | 12/06/30 | 7.50 |
| Royal Garden Blues | (COL 2884D) | 12/06/30 | 5.00 |
| White Jazz | (BRN 6092) | 3/24/31 | 7.50 |
| Maniac's Ball | (BRN 6242) | 12/18/31 | 5.00 |
| Smoke Rings | (BRN 6289) | 3/18/32 | 7.50 |
| Was I to Blame ...? | (BRN 6263) | 3/18/32 | 7.00 |
| Blue Jazz | (BRN 6358) | 7/25/32 | 5.00 |
| New Orleans | (BRN 6486) | 12/27/32 | 4.00 |
| Blue Prelude | (BRN 6513) | 1/31/33 | 4.00 |
| Under a Blanket of Blue | (BRN 6584) | 5/26/33 | 5.00 |
| Casa Loma Stomp | (BRN 7652) | 6/02/33 | 4.00 |
| It's the Talk of the Town | (BRN 6626) | 8/07/33 | 4.00 |
| A Study in Brown | (DEC 1159) | 2/04/37 | 3.50 |
| Smoke Rings | (DEC 1473) | 7/23/37 | 3.50 |
| Casa Loma Stomp | (DEC 1412) | 7/23/37 | 3.50 |
| Memories of You | | | |
| (Sonny Dunham) | (DEC 1672) | 12/01/37 | 3.50 |
| Sunrise Serenade (F. Carle) | (DEC 2321) | 2/17/39 | 3.00 |
| Rockin' Chair (L. Armstrong) | (DEC 2395) | 2/20/39 | 5.00 |
| No Name Jive (2 pts.) | (DEC 3089) | 3/18/40 | 4.00 |
| It's the Talk of the Town | (DEC 4292) | 1/15/42 | 3.00 |
| My Heart Tells Me | (DEC 18567) | 10/15/43 | 2.50 |

*The earliest designation on a record label indicating the change from Casa Loma Orchestra to Glen Gray and the Casa Loma Orchestra was in January, 1933 apparently.

**CAVALLARO, CARMEN**       NMP (.0-.75)

**CAVANAUGH TRIO, PAGE**       NMP (.0-.75)

**CHARIOTEERS, THE**       NMP (.0-.25)

**CHESTER, BOB**
Generally NMP except for these few discs:

| | | | |
|---|---|---|---|
| Aunt Hagar's Blues | (BLB 10513) | 10/12/39 | 2.50 |
| The Octave Jump | (BLB 10649) | 3/04/40 | 2.50 |

**Pee Wee Hunt, vocalist with Glen Gray**

Photograph courtesy Alf Hildman, West Des Moines

| | | | |
|---|---|---|---|
| Off the Record | (BLB 10865) | 8/01/40 | $ 2.50 |
| Flinging a Whing-Ding | (BLB 10964) | 9/24/40 | 2.50 |
| From Maine to California | (BLB 11313) | 9/25/41 | 2.50 |
| Harlem Confusion | (BLB 11384) | 10/28/41 | 2.50 |
| Sunburst (theme) | (BLB 11478) | 2/17/42 | 3.00 |
| Tanning Dr. Jekyll's Hide | (BLB 11521) | 3/04/42 | 2.50 |

## CHEVALIER, MAURICE*
Generally NMP with these exceptions:

| | | | |
|---|---|---|---|
| Louise | (VIC 21918) | 3/14/29 | 2.50 |
| Valentine | (VIC 22093) | 3/15/29 | 2.50 |
| You Brought a New Kind of Love to Me | (VIC 22405) | 4/04/30 | 2.50 |
| Mimi | (VIC 24063) | 6/29/32 | 2.50 |

*Only discs recorded in the U.S.A. are listed.

## CLARK, BUDDY
Generally NMP but for these vintage performances:

| | | | |
|---|---|---|---|
| Evening (with Gus Amheim) | (VIC 24061) | 7/02/32 | 7.50 |
| Stars Fell on Alabama (Freddy Martin) | (BRN 6976) | 9/14/34 | 5.00 |
| June in January | (MEL 13265) | 12/06/34 | 6.00 |
| Red Sails in the Sunset (L. Gluskin) | (BRN 7535) | 9/26/35 | 4.00 |
| Moon over Miami (L. Gluskin) | (BRN 7590) | 12/26/35 | 4.00 |
| The Glory of Love (N. Brandwynne) | (BRN 7660) | 4/13/36 | 2.00 |

(BRN, VOC, VIC, OKE sides 1936-41 in $3.00-2.00 range, as are COL 1946-47.)

## CLINTON, LARRY and his orchestra
Generally NMP but for the following sides:

| | | | |
|---|---|---|---|
| Midnight in the Madhouse (C. Spivak) | (VIC 25697) | 10/15/37 | 2.50 |
| Martha | (VIC 25789) | 2/11/38 | 3.00 |
| A Study in Blue | (VIC 25897) | 6/22/38 | 2.50 |

**Larry Clinton**              Photograph courtesy Alf Hildman, West Des Moines

| | | | |
|---|---|---|---|
| My Reverie | (VIC 26006) | 7/16/38 | $ 3.00 |
| Milenberg Joys | (VIC 26018) | 8/01/38 | 2.50 |
| Old Folks | (VIC 26056) | 9/01/38 | 3.00 |
| A Study in Green | (VIC 26137) | 12/23/38 | 2.50 |
| Deep Purple | (VIC 26141) | 12/23/38 | 3.00 |
| In a Persian Market | (VIC 26283) | 6/07/39 | 2.50 |
| A Study in Scarlet | (VIC 26435) | 7/14/39 | 2.50 |
| Study in Surrealism | (VIC 26481) | 1/02/40 | 2.50 |
| A Study in Modernism | (VIC 26582) | 3/27/40 | 2.50 |

**COBURN, JOLLY**                     NMP (.0-.50)

**COLE, NAT "KING"**

| | | | |
|---|---|---|---|
| Sweet Lorraine | (DEC 8520) | 12/06/40 | 4.00 |
| Honeysuckle Rose | (DEC 8535) | 12/06/40 | 4.00 |
| Early Morning Blues | (DEC 8541) | 3/14/41 | 4.00 |
| Scotchin' with the Soda | (DEC 8556) | 3/14/41 | 4.00 |
| Hit the Ramp | (DEC 8571) | 7/16/41 | 4.00 |
| I Like to Riff | (DEC 8592) | 7/16/41 | 4.00 |
| Call the Police | (DEC 8604) | 10/23/41 | 4.00 |
| Hit That Jive Jack | (DEC 8630) | 10/23/41 | 4.00 |
| Straighten Up and Fly Right | (CAP 154) | 11/30/43 | 2.50 |

| | | | |
|---|---|---|---|
| Sweet Lorraine | (CAP 20009) | 12/15/43 | $ 2.00 |
| It's Only a Paper Moon | (CAP 20012) | 12/15/43 | 2.50 |
| Body and Soul | (CAP 20010) | 1/17/44 | 2.00 |
| Sweet Georgia Brown | (CAP 239) | 5/23/45 | 2.00 |
| The Frim Fram Sauce | (CAP 224) | 10/11/45 | 2.00 |
| Route 66 | (CAP 256) | 3/15/46 | 2.50 |
| For Sentimental Reasons | (CAP 304) | 8/19/46 | 2.00 |
| The Christmas Song | (CAP 311) | 8/22/46 | 1.75 |
| You're the Cream in My Coffee | (CAP 10086) | 12/18/46 | 1.50 |

**COLEMAN, EMIL**                      NMP (.0-.50)

**COLUMBO, RUSS**
Generally NMP with six possible exceptions:

| | | | |
|---|---|---|---|
| I Don't Know Why | (VIC 22801) | 9/03/31 | 2.50 |
| Sweet and Lovely | (VIC 22802) | 9/09/31 | 2.00 |
| Goodnight, Sweetheart | (VIC 22826) | 10/09/31 | 2.00 |
| Prisoner of Love | (VIC 22867) | 10/09/31 | 2.50 |
| Paradise | (VIC 22976) | 4/06/32 | 2.00 |
| When You're in Love (with J. Grier) | (BRN 6972) | 8/31/34 | 2.50 |

**COMO, PERRY**                      NMP (.0-1.25)

**CONFREY, ZEZ**                      NMP (.0-.75)

**CONWAY'S BAND**                      NMP (.0-.10)

**COON-SANDERS ORCHESTRA**
Generally NMP for for:

| | | | |
|---|---|---|---|
| Some Little Bird | (COL A-3403) | 3/24/21 | 5.00 |
| Night Hawk Blues (theme) | (VIC 19316) | 4/05/24 | 4.00 |

**COURTNEY, DEL**                      NMP (.0-.25)

**CRAIG, FRANCIS**                      NMP (.0-.75)

**CRAWFORD, JESSIE**                      NMP (.0-.25)

## CROSBY, BING*

| | | | |
|---|---|---|---|
| I've Got the Girl (with A. Rinker) | (COL 824D) | 10/18/26 | $40.00 |
| Old Man River (P. Whiteman) | (VIC 21218) | 1/11/28 | 8.00 |
| Mississippi Mud (F. Trumbauer) | (OKE 40979) | 1/20/28 | 10.00 |
| 'Taint So, Honey, 'Taint So (Whiteman) | (COL 1444D) | 6/10/28 | 10.00 |
| I'm Crazy over You (S. Lanin) | (OKE 41228) | 1/25/29 | 10.00 |
| Let's Do It (Dorsey Bros.) | (OKE 41181) | 1/26/29 | 12.00 |
| My Kinda Love (Dorsey Bros.) | (OKE 41188) | 1/26/29 | 12.00 |
| Without a Song (Whiteman) | (COL 2023D) | 10/09/29 | 10.00 |
| I'm a Dreamer (Whiteman) | (COL 2010D) | 10/16/29 | 10.00 |
| After You've Gone (Whiteman) | (COL 2098D) | 10/18/29 | 12.00 |
| It Must Be True (G. Arnheim) | (VIC 22561) | 10/29/30 | 10.00 |
| The Little Things in Life (Arnheim) | (VIC 22580) | 11/25/30 | 8.00 |
| I Surrender Dear (Arnheim) | (VIC 22618) | 1/19/31 | 10.00 |
| Thanks to You (Arnheim) | (VIC 22700) | 3/02/31 | 10.00 |
| Just a Gigolo (Arnheim) | (VIC 22701) | 3/02/31 | 10.00 |
| Out of Nowhere | (BRN 6090) | 3/30/31 | 8.00 |
| Just One More Chance (V. Young) | (BRN 6120) | 5/04/31 | 8.00 |
| Gems from George White's Scandals (12″) | (BRN 20102) | 10/25/31 | 10.00 |
| Where the Blue of the Night Meets ... | (BRN 6226) | 11/23/31 | 15.00 |
| St. Louis Blues (D. Ellington) (12″) | (BRN 20105) | 2/11/32 | 15.00 |
| Face the Music Medley (12″) | (BRN 20106) | 3/08/32 | 15.00 |
| Lawd, You Made the Night Too Long (Boswells) | (BRN 20109) | 4/13/32 | 15.00 |
| Sweet Georgia Brown (Isham Jones) | (BRN 6320) | 4/23/32 | 8.00 |
| Please (Anson Weeks) | (BRN 6394) | 9/16/32 | 8.00 |
| Brother, Can You Spare a Dime? | (BRN 6414) | 10/25/32 | 8.00 |
| You're Getting to Be a Habit (G. Lombardo) | (BRN 6472) | 1/12/33 | 10.00 |

**Bing Crosby**                    Photograph courtesy RCA Victor

| | | | |
|---|---|---|---|
| My Honey's Lovin' Arms | | | |
| (Dorseys, Mills Bros.) | (BRN 6525) | 1/26/33 | $ 10.00 |
| Learn to Croon (J. Grier) | (BRN 6594) | 6/13/33 | 8.00 |
| Thanks | (BRN 6643) | 8/27/33 | 10.00 |
| Love Thy Neighbor | (BRN 6852) | 2/25/34 | 8.00 |
| Love in Bloom (I. Aaronson) | (BRN 6936) | 7/05/34 | 7.50 |

*Bing Crosby began to record for Decca in August, 1934. Price range for most of his Deccas from 1934-42 runs from $3.00-2.00.

## CROSBY, BOB and his orchestra
Generally NMP but for the few that follow:

| | | | |
|---|---|---|---|
| The Dixieland Band | (DEC 479) | 6/01/35 | 5.00 |
| Muskrat Ramble | (DEC 825) | 4/13/36 | 3.50 |
| Come Back, Sweet Papa | (DEC 896) | 6/12/36 | 3.50 |
| Sugar Foot Strut | (DEC 1094) | 6/12/36 | 3.50 |
| South Rampart Street Parade (12″) | (DEC 15038) | 11/16/37 | 7.50 |
| Yancey Special | (DEC 1747) | 3/10/38 | 3.00 |
| Big Crash from China (Bob Cats) | (DEC 1756) | 3/14/38 | 3.50 |
| Big Noise From Winnetka | | | |
| (Bob Cats) | (DEC 2208) | 10/14/38 | 5.00 |
| I'm Free (What's New?) | (DEC 2205) | 10/19/38 | 3.50 |
| Smokey Mary | (DEC 2569) | 1/23/39 | 3.00 |
| Spain (Bob Cats) | (DEC 3248) | 2/06/40 | 3.00 |
| Sugar Foot Stomp | (DEC 4390) | 1/27/42 | 3.00 |

## CRUMIT, FRANK                    NMP (.0-.20)

## CUGAT, XAVIER
Generally NMP but for these few:

| | | | |
|---|---|---|---|
| Caminito | (VIC 24387) | 8/15/33 | 3.50 |
| Hold Me Tight (Buddy Clark) | (VIC 25567) | 4/05/37 | 3.50 |
| The Thrill of a New Romance | | | |
| (Dinah Shore) | (VIC 26299) | 6/12/39 | 3.50 |
| Quiereme Mucho (D. Shore) | (VIC 26384) | 6/12/39 | 3.00 |
| The Breeze and I (D. Shore) | (VIC 26641) | 5/27/40 | 2.50 |
| Babalu (M. Valdez) | (COL 36048) | 3/14/41 | 2.00 |
| Chiu-Chiu (Lena Romay) | (COL 36651) | 7/20/42 | 1.75 |

**CUMMINS, BERNIE*** and his orchestra

| | | | |
|---|---|---|---|
| Ida | (GEN 5395) | 1/28/24 | $ 5.00 |
| St. Louis Blues | (GEN 5466) | 5/19/24 | 5.00 |
| Jiminy Gee | (GEN 5468) | 5/19/24 | 4.00 |
| Keep on Dancing | (GEN 5546) | 9/19/24 | 4.00 |
| Lonely Me | (GEN 5555) | 9/29/24 | 4.00 |
| Poplar Street Blues | (GEN 5641) | 1/22/25 | 4.50 |

*Cummins on BRN, VIC is generally NMP. His presence on the relatively rare GEN label accounts for listing him at all.

# D

**DAILEY, FRANK**                              NMP (.0-.50)

**DAVIS, MEYER** and his orchestra
Generally NMP except for this one item of interest:

| | | | |
|---|---|---|---|
| Honeymoon Hotel | | | |
| (Claude Thornhill on piano) | (COL 2816D) | 9/08/33 | 3.50 |

**DAWN, DOLLY**                              NMP (.0-.75)

**DELANGE, EDDIE** and his orchestra
Generally NMP with three possible exceptions:

| | | | |
|---|---|---|---|
| Copenhagen | (BLB 10027) | 10/18/38 | 2.00 |
| Muskrat Ramble | (BLB 10035) | 10/18/38 | 2.00 |
| Livery Stable Blues | (BLB 10094) | 12/17/38 | 2.00 |

**DELTA RHYTHM BOYS**                    NMP (.0-.50)

**DENNY, JACK**                              NMP (.0-.50)

**DIETRICH, MARLENE***
Generally NMP but for these:

| | | | |
|---|---|---|---|
| Falling in Love Again | (DEC 23141) | 12/11/39 | 4.00 |
| You Go to My Head | (DEC 23140) | 12/19/39 | 3.00 |

You Do Something to Me       (DEC 23139)    12/19/39 $ 2.50

\*Ms. Dietrich made her first record in 1928 in Berlin. But for a brief session in Los Angeles in November, 1934, she did not cut any sides in the U.S.A. until those cited above.

**DODDS, JOHNNY** and his various groups

| | | | |
|---|---|---|---|
| Oh Daddy | (PAR 12471) | 3/27 | 17.00 |
| Loveless Love | (PAR 12483) | 4/27 | 15.00 |
| San (Lil Armstrong) | (BRN 3574) | 4/21/27 | 15.00 |
| Oh! Lizzie (Lil Armstrong) | (BRN 3585) | 4/21/27 | 15.00 |
| Weary Blues (Bigard, Hines, Louis Armstrong) | (VOC 15632) | 4/22/27 | 50.00 |
| Wild Man Blues (Bigard, Hines, Armstrong) | (BRN 3567) | 4/22/27 | 25.00 |
| After You've Gone | (BRN 3568) | 10/08/27 | 15.00 |
| Blue Clarinet Stomp | (VIC 21554) | 7/05/28 | 7.00 |
| Bucktown Stomp | (VIC 38004) | 7/06/28 | 7.00 |
| Bull Fiddle Blues | (VIC 21552) | 7/06/28 | 7.00 |
| Sweet Lorraine (Lil Armstrong) | (VIC 38038) | 1/30/29 | 7.00 |
| My Little Isabel (Lil Armstrong) | (VIC 38541) | 1/30/29 | 7.00 |
| Goober Dance (Lil Armstrong) | (VIC 23396) | 2/07/29 | 7.00 |

**DONAHUE, AL**            NMP (.0-.75)

**DONAHUE, SAM** and his orchestra
Generally NMP with this interesting exception:

| | | | |
|---|---|---|---|
| It Counts a Lot (Count Basie on piano) | (OKE 6334) | 12/26/40 | 4.00 |

**DORNBERGER, CHARLES**       NMP (.0-.20)

**DORSEY BROTHERS ORCHESTRA\***

| | | | |
|---|---|---|---|
| Persian Rug | (OKE 40995) | 2/14/28 | $ 7.50 |
| The Spell of the Blues (Bing Crosby, G. Miller, E. Lang) | (OKE 41181) | 1/26/29 | 12.00 |
| My Kinda Love (Bing Crosby) | (OKE 41188) | 1/26/29 | 12.00 |
| Have a Little Faith in Me (Spanier, Bauduc) | (BAN 0571) | 1/13/30 | 8.00 |

| | | | |
|---|---|---|---|
| Ooh! That Kiss (Berigan, Miller) | (COL 2581D) | 12/09/31 | $ 7.50 |
| Someone Stole Gabriel's Horn | | | |
| (Berigan) | (BRN 01386) | 9/24/32 | 8.50 |
| Dr. Heckle and Mr. Jibe | | | |
| (Berigan, J. Mercer) | (BRN 01834) | 10/17/33 | 5.00 |
| Annie's Cousin Fanny | | | |
| (G. Miller vocal) | (BRN 6938) | 6/04/34 | 8.00 |
| By Heck | (DEC 118) | 8/14/34 | 4.00 |
| Stop, Look, and Listen | (DEC 208) | 8/15/34 | 4.00 |
| Milenberg Joys (C. Spivak, | | | |
| J. Stacy, Miller) | (DEC 119) | 8/23/34 | 4.00 |

*Periodically during the years 1929-34 the Dorseys recorded under the name "The Travelers" and, when sides were released on labels such as HAR and PHN, the orchestra was given a pseudonym, e.g., Jerry Mason, Harry Wilson, Paul Hamilton.

**DORSEY, JIMMY** and his orchestra
Generally NMP except for those given below:

| | | | |
|---|---|---|---|
| Parade of the Milk Bottle Caps | (DEC 941) | 7/07/36 | 3.00 |
| Pennies from Heaven Medley | | | |
| (Crosby, Armstrong, | | | |
| Langford) (12″) | (DEC 15027) | 8/17/36 | 4.00 |
| Peckin' (vocal by Bing Crosby) | (DEC 1301) | 3/03/37 | 4.00 |
| John Silver | (DEC 3334) | 4/29/38 | 3.00 |
| Six Lessons from Mme. LaZonga | (DEC 3152) | 4/09/40 | 2.50 |
| Contrasts (theme) | (DEC 3198) | 4/30/40 | 3.50 |
| I Understand | (DEC 3585) | 12/09/40 | 2.00 |
| Amapola | (DEC 3629) | 2/03/41 | 2.50 |
| Yours | (DEC 3657) | 2/03/41 | 2.50 |
| Green Eyes | (DEC 3698) | 3/19/41 | 2.50 |
| Time Was | (DEC 3859) | 5/19/41 | 2.00 |
| Fingerbustin' | (DEC 3928) | 5/19/41 | 2.00 |
| Arthur Murray Taught Me | | | |
| Dancing ... | (DEC 4122) | 12/10/41 | 2.50 |
| Tangerine | (DEC 4123) | 12/10/41 | 2.50 |

**Jimmy Dorsey**
Photograph courtesy Alf Hildman,
West Des Moines

**Lee Castle**
Photograph courtesy Val Air
Ballroom, West Des Moines

**Tommy Dorsey**

Photograph courtesy Alf Hildman,
West Des Moines

67

**DORSEY, TOMMY** and his orchestra/**Clambake Seven** (CS)

| | | | |
|---|---|---|---|
| You Are My Lucky Star (with Eleanor Powell) | (VIC 25158) | 10/11/35 | $ 3.50 |
| I'm Getting Sentimental over You (theme) | (VIC 25236) | 10/18/35 | 4.00 |
| The Music Goes 'Round and Around (CS) | (VIC 25201) | 12/09/35 | 4.00 |
| Song of India (B. Berigan) | (VIC 25523) | 1/29/37 | 2.50 |
| Stop, Look and Listen (12″) | (VIC 36207) | 4/15/37 | 4.00 |
| Boogie Woogie | (VIC 26054) | 9/16/38 | 2.50 |
| Hawaiian War Chant | (VIC 26126) | 11/29/38 | 2.50 |
| East of the Sun (F. Sinatra, B. Berigan) | (BLB 10726) | 4/23/40 | 3.50 |
| Without a Song (Sinatra) (12″) | (VIC 36396) | 1/20/41 | 4.00 |
| Swing Low, Sweet Chariot (12″) | (VIC 36399) | 2/17/41 | 4.00 |
| The Minor Goes Muggin' (Duke Ellington on piano) | (VIC 45-0002) | 5/14/45 | 3.50 |
| The Dorsey Concerto (with J. Dorsey) (12″, 2 pts.) | (VIC 46-0009) | 1/29/47 | 3.00 |

**DUCHIN, EDDY**          NMP (.0-1.00)

**DUNHAM, SONNY**
NMP but for his theme:

| | | | |
|---|---|---|---|
| Memories of You (small group) | (VAR 8234) | 3/40 | 3.50 |
| Memories of You (full band) | (BLB 11239) | 7/23/41 | 3.00 |

**DURBIN, DEANNA**          NMP (.0-.50)

**Tommy Dorsey**                    Photograph courtesy **RCA Victor**

# INTERMISSION 2

## *Labels to Look for*

As I admitted in my introductory remarks this *Guide* (Popular Section) huddles close to what one might call the common, non-esoteric record; the garden variety 78 generally found in private homes, second-hand stores, and thrift sales. I do not refer to Country-Western artists at all, and I touch incidentally only upon Jazz-Blues records *per se*. Still, I have it from reliable authorities that there is much market action for certain artists on certain labels, many of which fall into the Jazz-Blues realm (and most of which were recorded between 1920 and 1935). Just to keep you from making a terrible mistake I list below fifteen labels and numerous artists who are very attractive to collectors these days. Sift through your records one more time. If you come across any cited here set them aside, treat them gingerly, and think about what you wish to do. There are dealers who might be interested in your disc-overies.

**Autograph**
Merritt Brunies
Jelly Roll Morton
King Oliver

**Black Patti**
Katie Crippen
Fletcher Henderson
Alberta Hunter
James P. Johnson
Josie Miles
Julia Moody
Trixie Smith
Ethel Waters

**Brunswick**
Mildred Bailey
Bunny Berigan
Casa Loma
Bob Crosby
Frank Melrose
Red Nichols
Red Norvo
Ben Pollack
Sam Price
Louis Prima
Banjo Ikey Robinson
Artie Shaw
Omer Simeon
Jabbo Smith
Teddy Wilson

## Champion

Chicago Stompers
Turner Parrish
Wingy Manone
Frank Melrose
State Street Ramblers

## Columbia

Blue Ribbon Syncopaters
Oscar "Papa" Celestin
Cotton Club Orchestra
Fletcher Henderson
Maggie Jones
Bessie Smith
Clara Smith

## Emerson

Louisiana Five

## Gennett

Cook's Dreamland Orchestra
Fletcher Henderson
Jelly Roll Morton
King Oliver's Creole Jazz Band
Muggsy Spanier
New Orleans Rhythm Kings
Original Memphis Five
Red Onion Jazz Babies
Wolverines

## Harmony

Arkansas Travellers
Broadway Bell Hops
Dixie Stompers
Georgia Strutters
Mills Merry Makers
Phil Napoleon's Emperors

a. Silver-on-black Brunswick
(1936-39). Norvo record cut 1/21/38
b. Gold-on-red Columbia (1939-42).
This Heidt effort recorded 3/20/40

c. Gold-on-black Columbia
(1923-33). This record made 4/10/28

d. Decca gold-on-blue "perspective"
label (1934-37). This disc made
10/26/37
e. Silver-on-black Capitol (1942-47).
This Sherwood side made 5/5/42

| Melotone | Okeh |
|---|---|
| Charlie Barnet | Louis Armstrong |
| Blue Rhythm Boys | Perry Bradford |
| Connie's Inn Orchestra | Butterbeans and Susie |
| Frankie Franko | Benny Carter |
| Benny Goodman | Chicago Footwarmers |
| Wingy Manone | Chocolate Dandies |
| Adrian Rollini | Eddie Condon |
| Travellers | Dorsey Brothers |
| Washboard Rhythm Boys | Duke Ellington |
| | Troy Floyd |
| | Goofus Five |
| | Elizabeth Johnson |
| | Lonnie Johnson |
| | Richard M. Jones |
| | Bennie Moten |
| | New Orleans Feetwarmers |
| | Luis Russell |
| | Hazel Smith |
| | Hersal Thomas |
| | Frankie Trumbauer |
| | Sippie Wallace |
| | Clarence Williams |
| | Joe Venuti |

f. Gold-on-green Melotone
(1934-36). Haymes side cut 8/12/35
g. Gold-on-black oversize Okeh
(1928-32). First side by Dorseys cut
2/14/28

h. Gold-on-black Victor "scroll"
label (1926-37). This item cut
6/15/36
i. Red label Commodore (1938-44).
This 12" record cut 2/19/44

72

**Paramount**

Lovie Austin's Serenaders
Jimmy Blythe
Junie Cobb's Hometown Band
Ida Cox
Charlie "Cow Cow" Davenport
Will Ezell
Fletcher Henderson
Freddie Keppard and His Jazz
   Cardinals
Meade Lux Lewis
Jelly Roll Morton
Jimmy O'Bryant's Washboard
   Wizards
King Oliver's Jazz Band
Ma Rainey
Trixie Smith

**Perfect**

Henry Allen
Cab Calloway
Chicago Loopers
Buddy Christian's Jazz Rippers
Duke Ellington's Washingtonians
Fletcher Henderson
Baron Lee and His Blue Rhythm
   Band
Original Memphis Five
Ben Pollack
The Redheads
Whoopee Makers
Joe Valenti

**QRS**

Clarence Williams Orchestra
Earl Hines

**Victor**

Henry Allen
Bix Beiderbecke
Johnny Dodds and His Orchestra
Paul Howard's Quality Serenaders
McKinney's Cotton Pickers
Bubber Miley
Jelly Roll Morton's Red Hot
   Peppers
Bennie Moten
Mound City Blue Blowers
King Oliver's Orchestra
Fats Waller
Washboard Rhythm Kings

k

l

j

j. Black "arch" Victor in vogue
1908-26. This Whiteman disc cut
3/19/20
k. Blue-on-cream Bluebird
(1933-37). This item recorded 7/3/36
l. Gold-on-dark-blue Bluebird
(1938-42). This disc made 2/13/40

73

# DUKE ELLINGTON

Photographs
courtesy  RCA Victor

Photograph courtesy
Val Air Ballroom, West Des Moines

# E

**ECKSTINE, BILLY**     NMP (.0-1.25)

**ELLINGTON, DUKE*** and his various orchestras

| | | | |
|---|---|---|---|
| Choo Choo (as the "Washingtonians") | (BLU 1002) | 11/24 | $ 40.00 |
| Trombone Blues | (PAT 36333) | 9/25 | 30.00 |
| Georgia Grind | (PAT 7504) | 3/26 | 30.00 |
| Wanna-Go-Back-Again Blues | (GEN 3291) | 3/20/26 | 20.00 |
| Animal Crackers | (GEN 3342) | 6/21/26 | 20.00 |
| East St. Louis Toodle-Oo | (VOC 1064) | 11/29/26 | 15.00 |
| Immigration Blues | (VOC 1077) | 12/29/26 | 15.00 |
| New Orleans Low-Down | (VOC 1086) | 2/03/27 | 15.00 |
| East St. Louis Toodle-Oo | (BRN 3480) | 3/14/27 | 12.00 |
| Black and Tan Fantasy | (BRN 3526) | 4/07/27 | 20.00 |
| Creole Love Call | (VIC 21137) | 10/26/27 | 10.00 |
| Black and Tan Fantasy | (OKE 8521) | 11/03/27 | 20.00 |
| Red Hot Band | (VOC 1153) | 12/29/27 | 15.00 |
| Jubilee Stomp | (OKE 41013) | 1/19/28 | 5.00 |
| Diga Diga Doo | (OKE 8602) | 7/10/28 | 7.00 |
| Black Beauty | (OKE 8636) | 10/01/28 | 8.00 |
| The Mooche | (OKE 8623) | 10/01/28 | 10.00 |
| Ring Dem Bells | (VIC 22528) | 9/26/30 | 7.00 |
| Mood Indigo | (VIC 22587) | 12/10/30 | 7.00 |
| Rockin' Chair | (ORL 2191) | 1/10/31 | 7.00 |
| Creole Rhapsody (2 pts.) | (VIC 36049) | 6/11/31 | 10.00 |
| St. Louis Blues (Bing Crosby) | (BRN 20105) | 2/11/32 | 15.00 |
| Solitude | (BRN 6987) | 9/12/34 | 7.00 |
| Sophisticated Lady (piano solo) | (BRN 7990) | 12/21/36 | 7.50 |
| Concerto for Cootie | (VIC 26598) | 3/15/40 | 3.50 |
| Never No Lament (Don't Get Around Much ...) | (VIC 26610) | 5/04/40 | 3.00 |
| Take the "A" Train (theme) | (VIC 27380) | 2/15/41 | 2.50 |
| I Got It Bad (and That Ain't Good) | (VIC 27531) | 6/26/41 | 2.50 |
| Perdido | (VIC 27880) | 1/21/42 | 2.50 |
| The "C" Jam Blues | (VIC 27856) | 1/21/42 | 2.50 |

Black, Brown, and Beige (12″)     (VIC 29-0400)  12/11/44  $ 6.00

*Ellington's record production, 1924-47, was so vast I cannot list but a fraction of his output. The prices given are meant to be broadly representative. Obviously the pre-1940 discs are more valuable relatively.

**ELMAN ZIGGY**                      NMP (.0-1.00)

**ENNIS, SKINNAY**                   NMP (.0-.25)

**EUROPE, JIM** and his orchestra/**369th Inf. Band**

| | | | |
|---|---|---|---|
| Down Home Rag | (VIC 35359) | 12/19/13 | 50.00 |
| El Irresistible | (VIC 35360) | 12/19/13 | 50.00 |
| Castle House Rag | (VIC 35372) | 2/10/14 | 45.00 |
| Castle Walk | (VIC 17553) | 2/10/14 | 45.00 |
| Broadway Hit Medley | (PAT 22082) | 3/19 | 35.00 |
| St. Louis Blues | (PAT 22087) | 3/19 | 35.00 |
| Arabian Nights | (PAT 20080) | 3/19 | 30.00 |
| Darktown Strutters' Ball | (PAT 22081) | 3/19 | 35.00 |
| Hesitation Blues   (Noble Sissle) | (PAT 22086) | 3/07/19 | 25.00 |
| Memphis Blues | (PAT 22085) | 3/07/19 | 30.00 |
| Russian Rag | (PAT 22087) | 3/07/19 | 25.00 |
| Mirandy | (PAT 22089) | 3/14/19 | 25.00 |
| Jazz Baby | (PAT 22103) | 3/14/19 | 25.00 |
| Jazzola | (PAT 22104) | 3/14/19 | 25.00 |
| That's Got 'Em | (PAT 22146) | 5/07/19 | 20.00 |
| Clarinet Marmalade | (PAT 22167) | 5/07/19 | 20.00 |
| Missouri Blues | (PAT 22147) | 5/07/19 | 20.00 |

# F

**FAYE, ALICE**

Generally NMP but, for the curiosity value, these at:

Honeymoon Hotel
(Rudy Vallee orch.)            (BLB 5171)    9/06/33    3.00

**Skinnay Ennis**            Photograph courtesy Alf Hildman, West Des Moines

| | | | |
|---|---|---|---|
| Here's the Key To My Heart | | | |
| (Freddy Martin orch.) | (COL CL-3608) | 7/13/34 | $ 2.50 |
| My Future Star | (MEL 13220) | 9/26/34 | 2.50 |
| According to the Moonlight | (MEL 13346) | 2/26/35 | 2.50 |
| I'm Shooting High | (ARC 6-03-08) | 1/04/36 | 3.00 |
| Goodnight, My Love | (BRN 7821) | 12/06/36 | 3.00 |
| This Year's Kisses | (BRN 7825) | 1/24/37 | 3.00 |
| Never in a Million Years | (BRN 7860) | 3/18/37 | 3.00 |

**FIELDS, SHEP*** and his orchestras          NMP (.0-1.25)

*Fields presents one of those dilemmas that is difficult to resolve without alienating someone. His sides on BLB (1936-42) are not in demand in any broad sense. Yet there are collectors who track down and pay handsomely for every Fields' disc they can find, especially those released on the blue-yellow BLB label in fashion from 1933-37. By and large, however, most people will not pay more than $1.50 for a Fields' record for a very simple reason — they cannot think of a reason why they should. Fields made no unique contribution to the dance band era, nor were any of his discs particularly memorable. I find it ironic that Fields' best band (1941-42) came too late to displace the Rippling Rhythm sound in the public imagination. Perhaps his "New Music," non-brass orchestra of 1941-42 will someday gain the retroactive recognition it deserves. Until that time, Fields remains NMP.

**FIORITO, TED**                          NMP (.0-.50)

**FISHER, FREDDIE**
**"SCHNICKELFRITZ"**                     NMP (.0-.10)

**FITZGERALD, ELLA** and her various groups
Generally NMP with these possible exceptions:

| | | | |
|---|---|---|---|
| My Last Affair (Chick Webb) | (DEC 1061) | 11/18/36 | 3.50 |
| Organ Grinder's Swing | | | |
| (Chick Webb) | (DEC 1062) | 11/18/36 | 3.50 |
| Big Boy Blue (Mills Bros.) | (DEC 1148) | 1/14/37 | 3.00 |
| I'm Beginning to See the Light | | | |
| (Ink Spots) | (DEC 23399) | 2/26/45 | 2.50 |

**Shep Fields**          Photograph courtesy Alf Hildman, West Des Moines

**Ted Fio Rito**        Photograph courtesy Alf Hildman, West Des Moines

81

| | | | |
|---|---|---|---|
| It's Only a Paper Moon | | | |
| (Delta Rhythm Boys) | (DEC 23425) | 3/27/45 | $ 2.50 |
| The Frim Fram Sauce | | | |
| (Louis Armstrong) | (DEC 23496) | 1/18/46 | 2.50 |
| It's a Pity to Say Goodnight | | | |
| (D. Rhythm Boys) | (DEC 23670) | 8/29/46 | 2.00 |
| Sentimental Journey | | | |
| (Eddie Heywood) | (DEC 23844) | 1/24/47 | 2.00 |
| A Sunday Kind of Love | | | |
| (Bobby Haggart) | (DEC 23866) | 3/19/47 | 2.00 |
| Flying Home (Vic Schoen orch.) | (DEC 23956) | 10/04/47 | 2.00 |

**FOMEEN, BASIL**　　　　　　　NMP (.0-.20)

**FOSTER, CHUCK**　　　　　　NMP (.0-.25)

**FOX, ROY**　　　　　　　　　NMP (.0-.50)

**FROEBA, FRANK** and his Swing Band
　Generally NMP. There are three items of possible interest:

| | | | |
|---|---|---|---|
| Just to Be in Caroline (Berigan) | (COL 3131D) | 4/17/36 | 2.50 |
| Organ Grinder's Swing | | | |
| (Berigan, Marsala) | (COL 3151D) | 8/27/36 | 2.50 |
| It All Begins and Ends with You | | | |
| (Berigan) | (COL 3152D) | 8/27/36 | 2.50 |

**FROMAN, JANE**

| | | | |
|---|---|---|---|
| Sharing | (VIC 22461) | 6/10/30 | 5.00 |
| I Only Have Eyes for You | (BRN 01927) | 9/14/34 | 4.00 |
| Lost in a Fog | (BRN 01902) | 9/14/34 | 4.00 |
| If You Love Me | (DEC 725) | 2/13/36 | 2.50 |
| Please Believe Me | (DEC 710) | 2/13/36 | 2.50 |

**FRY, CHARLIE**　　　　　　　NMP (.0-.25)

**FUNK, LARRY** and his Band of a Thousand Melodies
　Generally NMP but for these few interesting sides:

| | | | |
|---|---|---|---|
| Rain (vocal by Vaughn Monroe) | (BAN 33219) | 9/19/34 | 3.00 |
| Too Beautiful for Words | | | |
| (V. Monroe) | (BAN 33237) | 9/19/34 | 3.00 |

# G

**GARBER, JAN**                                    NMP (.0-1.00)

**GARLAND, JUDY**
   Generally NMP with these modest exceptions:

| | | | |
|---|---|---|---|
| Stompin' at the Savoy | | | |
| (Bob Crosby orch.) | (DEC 848) | 6/12/36 | $ 3.00 |
| You Made Me Love You | | | |
| (Dear Mr. Gable) | (DEC 1463) | 9/24/37 | 3.00 |
| Over the Rainbow | (DEC 2672) | 7/28/39 | 3.00 |
| Friendship (with Johnny Mercer) | (DEC 3165) | 4/15/40 | 2.50 |
| For Me and My Gal | | | |
| (with Gene Kelly) | (DEC 18480) | 7/26/42 | 2.00 |

**GOLDKETTE, JEAN** and his orchestras
   Generally NMP but for this brief line of sides:

| | | | |
|---|---|---|---|
| My Sweetheart | | | |
| (with the Dorseys in band) | (VIC 19313) | 3/27/24 | 3.00 |
| It's the Blues (Dorseys) | (VIC 19600) | 3/27/24 | 3.00 |
| Dinah (J. Dorsey, J. Venuti) | (VIC 19947) | 1/28/26 | 2.50 |
| Hush-a-Bye (B. Beiderbecke, | | | |
| F. Trumbauer) | (VIC 20270) | 10/12/26 | 3.00 |
| Sunday | | | |
| (Beiderbecke, Trumbauer) | (VIC 20273) | 10/15/26 | 3.00 |
| I'm Looking over a Four-Leaf | | | |
| Clover (Beiderbecke) | (VIC 20466) | 1/28/27 | 2.00 |
| I'm Gonna Meet My Sweetie Now | | | |
| (Beiderbecke) | (VIC 20675) | 1/31/27 | 2.50 |
| Look at the World and Smile | | | |
| (Beiderbecke, E. Lang) | (VIC 20472) | 2/01/27 | 2.00 |
| Slow River (Beiderbecke) | (VIC 20926) | 5/06/27 | 2.50 |
| Blue River (Beiderbecke, | | | |
| Lang, Venuti) | (VIC 20981) | 9/15/27 | 2.50 |
| My Ohio Home (Hoagy | | | |
| Carmichael vocal, piano) | (VIC 21166) | 12/12/27 | 3.00 |

**GOODMAN, AL**                                 NMP (.0-.50)

## GOODMAN, BENNY and his orchestras/combos

| | | | |
|---|---|---|---|
| Wolverine Blues (with G. Miller) | (VOC 15656) | 1/23/28 | $ 20.00 |
| Jungle Blues | | | |
|    (T. Dorsey, B. Pollack) | (BRN 4013) | 6/04/28 | 10.00 |
| Shirt Tail Stomp | | | |
|    (T. Dorsey, Pollack) | (BRN 3975) | 6/04/28 | 10.00 |
| Clarinetitis | (VOC 15705) | 6/13/28 | 10.00 |
| Muskrat Scramble (sic) | | | |
|    (W. Manone, Joe Sullivan) | (BRN 4968) | 8/13/29 | 8.00 |
| What Have We Got to Do Tonight | | | |
|    (Miller, Bauduc, Lang) | (MEL 12138) | 3/18/31 | 8.00 |
| Slow But Sure (Berigan, | | | |
|    T. Dorsey, Krupa, Lang) | (MEL 12205) | 6/20/31 | 8.00 |
| Help Yourself to Happiness | | | |
|    (Miller) | (COL 2542D) | 9/18/31 | 8.00 |
| I Gotta Right to Sing the Blues | | | |
|    (J. Teagarden, Krupa) | (COL 2835D) | 10/18/33 | 10.00 |
| Texas Tea Party (Teagarden) | (COL 2845D) | 10/27/33 | 8.00 |
| Junk Man (M. Bailey, | | | |
|    C. Hawkins, Krupa) | (COL 2892D) | 2/02/34 | 10.00 |
| Bugle Call Rag | | | |
|    (Thornhill on piano) | (COL 2958D) | 8/16/34 | 8.00 |
| Like a Bolt from the Blue | | | |
|    (Buddy Clark) | (COL 2988D) | 11/26/34 | 5.00 |
| Music Hall Rag | (COL 3011D) | 11/26/34 | 5.00 |
| Down Home Rag | (COL 3033D) | 1/15/35 | 5.00 |
| I'm Livin' in a Great Big Way | | | |
|    (Buddy Clark) | (VIC 25011) | 4/04/35 | 5.00 |
| Hunkadola | (VIC 25009) | 4/04/35 | 5.00 |
| King Porter | (VIC 25090) | 7/01/35 | 3.00 |
| Body and Soul (Trio) | (VIC 25115) | 7/13/35 | 3.00 |
| Stompin' at the Savoy | (VIC 25247) | 1/24/36 | 3.00 |
| Sing, Sing, Sing (12″) | (VIC 36205) | 7/06/37 | 5.00 |
| Don't Be That Way | (VIC 25792) | 2/16/38 | 3.00 |
| And the Angels Sing | (VIC 26170) | 2/01/39 | 2.50 |

| | | | |
|---|---|---|---|
| Jumpin' at the Woodside (arr. by C. Basie) | (COL 35210) | 8/10/39 | $ 4.00 |
| Flying Home (F. Henderson on piano) (Sextet) | (COL 35254) | 10/02/39 | 3.50 |
| Let's Dance (theme) | (COL 35301) | 10/24/39 | 3.00 |
| Just like Taking Candy . . . (F. Astaire, L. Hampton) | (COL 35517) | 5/09/40 | 4.00 |
| Henderson Stomp (Henderson on piano) | (COL 35820) | 11/13/40 | 4.00 |
| Clarinet a la King | (OKE 6544) | 10/23/41 | 3.50 |
| Jersey Bounce | (OKE 6590) | 1/23/42 | 3.50 |
| Why Don't You Do Right? (Peggy Lee) | (COL 36652) | 7/27/42 | 3.00 |
| Gotta Be This or That (2 pts.) | (COL 36813) | 4/27/45 | 2.50 |
| Oh Baby (12″, 2 pts.) | (COL 55039) | 5/14/46 | 3.00 |
| It Takes Time (Johnny Mercer vocal) | (CAP 376) | 3/47 | 3.00 |
| How High the Moon (Septet) | (CAP 20126) | 4/17/47 | 3.00 |

**GOODRICH ORCHESTRA**     NMP (.0-.25)

**GORDON, GRAY**     NMP (.0-.50)

**GRACE, TEDDY**     NMP (.0-1.00)

**GRANT, BOB**     NMP (.0-.10)

**GRAY, GLEN**     (see CASA LOMA ORCHESTRA)

**GREEN, JOHNNY** and his orchestra
  Certainly NMP, but these are worthy:

| | | | |
|---|---|---|---|
| Easy Come, Easy Go (vocal Lee Wiley) | (BRN 6855) | 3/17/34 | 3.00 |
| An Earful of Music (Ethel Merman) | (BRN 6995) | 10/08/34 | 2.50 |
| Top Hat, White Tie and Tails (F. Astaire) | (BRN 7487) | 6/27/35 | 4.00 |

**GRIER, JIMMY**     NMP (.0-1.25)

# INTERMISSION 3

## *What's in a Name?*

Sooner or later, the 78 rpm record enthusiast encounters terminology. The long history of disc records is complex, intriguing, and replete with technical language. Since records and record-playing machines are as close as Siamese twins there has always been a lexical overlap, which generates some confusion in the ranks of contemporary record collectors. There is neither time nor space here to unravel the etymology of a century of record-related terms (e.g., ''phonautograph,'' ''microphonograph'') but it might prove useful to you to master a few key definitions. The names given below are sufficiently common still to warrant special attention. Every month someone runs across the word ''graphophone'' and asks me what it was intended to mean (a label, a company, a machine?). Perhaps this brief review will lend some historical-linguistic perspective to this fascinating adjunct to record collecting.

### *Phonograph*

A resilient term employed (but not coined) by Thomas Edison to describe the hand-operated talking machine he and assistant John Kruesi invented in 1877 and which was patented in February, 1878. The Edison phonograph was intended to play ''cylinders'' (although he produced a disc machine in October, 1913) which he continued to manufacture until 1929, long after the public switched allegiance to disc records. The term also appeared in corporate titles (North American Phonograph Company, Columbia Phonograph Company, for example). Eventually, "phonograph" became a generic word, meaning *all* record-playing devices, and is still used by many of us as an inclusive descriptor.

### *Graphophone*

The name given by Chichester Bell and Charles Tainter to their patented (May, 1886) variation of the phonograph. Refinements included an improved wax-covered cardboard cylinder, electric motor, and flexible stylus. Marketed originally by the American Graphophone Company (1887) this apparatus went into decline after 1903 and lost its broad appeal completely by 1914, despite the disc adaptor available from 1902 on.

### *Gramophone*

The name conceived by Emile Berliner and given (1887) to his talking machine. Berliner's piece departed from the phonograph-graphophone in one very significant regard: it serviced laterally-cut discs instead of the familiar cylinders. Early 7" "plates" rotated, with manual assistance, at 70 rpm. Berliner formed the U.S. Gramophone Company in 1893. It was the Improved Gramophone that Francis Barraud used as a (second) model in the *His Master's Voice* painting. Overseas, the term "gramophone" was never dislodged by "phonograph," as it was in the U.S.A.

## *Zonophone*

A description concocted by entrepreneur Frank Seaman to designate a heavier, more ornate version of the Improved Gramophone, which he attempted to market at home and abroad (1901) as competition to the Gramophone interests. Zonophone's baby-blue label discs (very rare) were supposed to rival Gramophone's red label records and featured artists such as Enrico Caruso (1902). Zonophone was bought out in 1903 by the Gramophone people but the Zonophone label was in evidence until the 1930s.

## *Victrola*

The Victor Talking Machine Company was founded in 1901. In 1905 chief executive Eldridge Johnson set out to perfect the physical appearance of the gramophones of the period and developed (1906) a console which would blend well with home furniture. The flared horn was eliminated and the turntable-stylus assembly was hidden within the wooden cabinet. Johnson called this property the ''Victrola'' and marketed it initially at $200. Later it was made available in table models. Columbia countered with the ''Grafonola'' but Victor's dominance was not seriously challenged until the 1920s. Countless Americans still refer to their modern record-players as ''Victrolas,'' clear testimony to the power of an original idea.

There are many other fugitive terms we might explore (''Radiola,'' ''Neophone,'' ''Panatrope,'' ''Pathephone,'' e.g.) but none linger in the air like the five mentioned above. The talking machine's first thirty years (1887-1917) were dynamic, productive, and controversial. Men fought bitterly for control of an idea whose destiny they could not define or envision precisely. The snowstorm of trade names peculiar to that era is a manifestation of the creativity that abounded, and is worthy of a respectful, retroactive bow. A phonograph is a phonograph is a phonograph, whatever the year and whatever the model.

Gold-on-blue Vocalion (1937-40).
This disc recorded 3/18/40

Sources for further reading: Roland Gelatt, *The Fabulous Phonograph, 1877-1977,* (Collier; New York; 1977); *High Fidelity* (January, 1977); *Saturday Review* (July 23, 1977); Schwann *Record and Tape Guide* (September, 1977); *Stereo Review* (July, 1977), 62-65; Oliver Read and Walter L. Welch, *From Tin Foil to Stereo* (H.W. Sams; Indianapolis; 1976).

**Marion Hutton**          Photograph courtesy Alf Hildman, West Des Moines

# H

**HACKETT, BOBBY** and his orchestra

| | | | |
|---|---|---|---|
| At the Jazz Band Ball (Condon, Brunies, P.W. Russell) | (VOC 4047) | 2/16/38 | $ 4.00 |
| That Da-Da Strain | (VOC 4142) | 2/16/38 | 4.00 |
| A Ghost of a Chance (Condon, Caceres, P.W. Russell) | (VOC 4565) | 11/04/38 | 4.00 |
| Poor Butterfly | (VOC 4499) | 11/04/38 | 4.00 |
| Ain't Misbehavin' | (VOC 4877) | 4/13/39 | 3.50 |
| Sunrise Serenade | (VOC 4806) | 4/13/39 | 3.50 |
| That Old Gang of Mine (F. Carle) | (VOC 5620) | 1/25/40 | 3.00 |
| Clarinet Marmalade (F. Carle) | (VOC 5493) | 1/25/40 | 3.00 |

**HALL, GEORGE***  NMP (.0-.75)

 *It matters not in terms of value, but the collector probably should know that Dolly Dawn (q.v.) joined Hall's band as a vocalist in 1935 and was allowed to make records with his orchestra under the name ''Dolly Dawn and Her Dawn Patrol'' band until late 1941.

**HALLETT, MAL**  NMP (.0-.50)

**HALSTEAD, HENRY**  NMP (.0-.25)

**HAMP, JOHNNY**  NMP (.0-1.00)

**HAMPTON, LIONEL** and his various groups
Generally NMP with these likely exceptions:

| | | | |
|---|---|---|---|
| Jivin' the Vibres (Krupa, Elman) | (VIC 25535) | 2/08/37 | 4.00 |
| Stompology (Hodges, Stacy, J. Kirby, Mezzrow) | (VIC 25601) | 4/14/37 | 4.00 |
| China Stomp (Hodges, Kirby, C. Cole) | (VIC 25586) | 4/26/37 | 4.00 |
| After You've Gone (Elman, Musso, Stacy) | (VIC 25674) | 9/05/37 | 4.00 |
| Ring Dem Bells (C. Williams, Hodges, Stacy) | (VIC 26017) | 1/18/38 | 4.00 |
| Shoe Shiner's Drag (H. James, B. Carter, Kirby) | (VIC 26011) | 7/21/38 | 3.50 |

| | | | |
|---|---|---|---|
| Memories of You (R. Stewart, H. Carney, L. Brown) | (VIC 26304) | 6/13/39 | $ 3.50 |
| Early Session Hop (Gillespie, Carter, Berry, Hawkins) | VIC 26393) | 9/11/39 | 4.00 |
| Dinah (Carter, Singleton, E. Hall, Hawkins) | (VIC 26557) | 12/21/39 | 4.00 |
| Flying Home (Elman, Mondello, N. Fatool) | (VIC 26595) | 2/26/40 | 4.00 |
| Jack the Bellboy (Nat Cole, Oscar Moore) | (VIC 26652) | 5/10/40 | 4.00 |
| Flying Home (theme) | (DEC 18394) | 5/26/42 | 2.50 |
| Hamp's Boogie Woogie | (DEC 18613) | 3/02/44 | 2.50 |
| Hey-Ba-Ba-Re-Bop | (DEC 18754) | 12/01/45 | 2.00 |
| Air Mail Special (2 pts.) | (DEC 18880) | 1/30/46 | 2.50 |

**HAPPINESS BOYS, THE**  NMP (.0-.50)

**HARING, BOB**  NMP (.0-.50)

**HARMONICATS, THE**  NMP (.0-.75)

**HARRIS, PHIL**  NMP (.0-.50)

**HAWKINS, COLEMAN*** and his various groups

| | | | |
|---|---|---|---|
| Jamaica Shout (Higginbotham, Kirby) | (OKE 41566) | 9/29/33 | 5.00 |
| It Sends Me | (PHN 1837) | 3/08/34 | 3.50 |
| On the Sunny Side of the Street | (PHN 1825) | 3/08/34 | 3.50 |
| Body and Soul (theme) | (BLB 10253) | 10/11/39 | 3.50 |
| Dedication | (CMD 533) | 5/25/40 | 3.50 |
| Esquire Bounce (Tatum, Pettiford, E. Hall, Catlett) | (CMD 547) | 12/04/43 | 4.00 |
| Crazy Rhythm (E. Heywood, Pettiford, Manne) | (SIG 28104) | 12/23/43 | 4.00 |
| Sweet Lorraine (12″) (Heywood, Manne) | (SIG 90001) | 12/23/43 | 4.50 |
| Imagination (T. Wilson, Cozy Cole) | (KEY 612) | 2/17/44 | 3.50 |

| | | | |
|---|---|---|---|
| Louise (12″) (Byas, Guarnieri) | (KEY 1308) | 5/24/44 | $ 4.00 |
| Three Little Words (12″) | (KEY 1316) | 5/24/44 | 4.00 |
| Make Believe (12″) | | | |
| (Kirby, Catlett, Wilson) | (KEY 1317) | 5/29/44 | 4.00 |
| Hallelujah (12″) | (KEY 1320) | 5/29/44 | 4.00 |
| It's the Talk of the Town | (CAP 205) | 3/09/45 | 2.50 |
| Say It Isn't So | (VIC 40-0131) | 10/03/46 | 2.50 |

*In the period 1934-38 Hawkins cut a number of records in overseas locations such as London, Paris, The Hague on labels including HMV, DEC, PHN, PAN, and VOC. These foreign sides are rather rare and bring very high prices among some collectors. It would be well to watch for these uncommon records.

## HAWKINS, ERSKINE and his orchestra
Generally NMP with these early exceptions:

| | | | |
|---|---|---|---|
| I Can't Escape from You | | | |
| (Billy Daniels vocal) | (VOC 3280) | 7/20/36 | 3.50 |
| Without a Shadow of a Doubt | (VOC 3289) | 7/20/36 | 3.50 |
| Coquette (B. Daniels) | (VOC 3318) | 9/08/36 | 3.50 |
| Swinging in Harlem | (VOC 3336) | 9/08/36 | 3.50 |
| Dear Old Southland | (VOC 3567) | 4/19/37 | 3.50 |
| Uproar Shout | (VOC 3545) | 4/19/37 | 3.50 |
| I'll See You in My Dreams | (VOC 3689) | 8/12/37 | 3.50 |
| I Found a New Baby | (VOC 3668) | 8/12/37 | 3.50 |
| Who's Sorry Now? | (VOC 4072) | 2/25/38 | 3.00 |
| Lost in the Shuffle | (VOC 4007) | 2/25/38 | 3.00 |
| After Hours | (BLB 10879) | 6/10/40 | 3.00 |
| Bicycle Bounce | (BLB 11547) | 5/27/42 | 3.00 |
| Tippin' In (theme) | (VIC 20-1639) | 1/10/45 | 3.00 |

## HAYMES, DICK                    TIP (.0-1.50)

## HAYMES, JOE*                    NMP (.0-1.50)

*Early sides by Haymes' orchestra (1932-35) on VIC, MEL, BAN, COL, PER, and BLB are reasonably interesting from a musical standpoint and probably deserve a $2 price tag. Not much he did on ARC is worth collecting.

**HEIDT, HORACE\***          NMP (.0-1.00)

  \*At one time or another between 1937 and 1942 Heidt featured such persons as Frankie Carle, Alvino Rey, The King Sisters, Gordon McRae, Art Carney, Bobby Hackett, and Fred Lowry. Unfortunately the music he chose to record was not as memorable and interests very few collectors today.

**HENDERSON, FLETCHER\*** and his various groups

| | | | |
|---|---|---|---|
| The Unknown Blues (piano solo) | (BSW 2026) | 9/21 | $45.00 |
| Chime Blues (piano solo) | (BSW 2116) | 3/23 | 45.00 |
| Beale Street Mama | (PAR 20226) | 5/01/23 | 35.00 |
| Down Hearted Blues | (PAR 20235) | 5/23 | 30.00 |
| When You Walked Out ... | (PAR 20239) | 5/23 | 30.00 |
| Gulf Coast Blues | (COL A-3951) | 6/07/23 | 20.00 |
| My Sweetie Went Away | (PAR 20251) | 6/25/23 | 30.00 |
| Gulf Coast Blues | (VOC 14636) | 6/28/23 | 15.00 |
| Dicty Blues | (VOC 14654) | 8/09/23 | 15.00 |
| Down South Blues | (VOC 14691) | 10/06/23 | 15.00 |
| Charleston Crazy (as the "Seven Brown Babies") | (AJX 17011) | 10/23 | 25.00 |
| Do Doodle Dom (as the "Seven Brown Babies") | (AJX 17009) | 10/23 | 25.00 |
| You've Got to Get Hot | (VOC 14726) | 10/27/23 | 20.00 |
| 31st Street Blues | (PAT 036042) | 11/26/23 | 15.00 |
| Linger Awhile | (EDI 51277) | 11/27/23 | 20.00 |
| Chattanooga | (AJX 17017) | 12/23 | 25.00 |
| Bull Blues | (AJX 17016) | 12/23 | 25.00 |
| Oh! Sister, Ain't That Hot? | (EMR 17013) | 1/24 | 15.00 |
| War Horse Blues | (BRN 2592) | 3/11/24 | 12.00 |
| Tea Pot Dome Blues | (VOC 14800) | 4/15/24 | 15.00 |
| Somebody Stole My Gal | (COL 126D) | 4/16/24 | 15.00 |
| Feeling the Way I Do | (BAN 1364) | 5/06/24 | 15.00 |
| Manda (Louis Armstrong) | (COL 228D) | 10/07/24 | 15.00 |
| My Rose Marie (Armstrong, Hawkins, Redman) | (PAT 036156) | 10/13/24 | 15.00 |
| Shanghai Shuffle | (PAT 036157) | 10/13/24 | 15.00 |

| | | | |
|---|---|---|---|
| One of These Days | (BAN 1457) | 11/10/24 | $ 15.00 |
| Naughty Man | (COL 249D) | 11/14/24 | 15.00 |
| Everybody Loves My Baby (Armstrong) | (DOM 3444) | 11/24/24 | 17.50 |
| Prince of Wails | (PAR 20367) | 12/24/24 | 17.50 |
| Alabamy Bound | (BAN 1488) | 1/30/25 | 15.00 |
| Memphis Bound | (VOC 15030) | 4/18/25 | 17.50 |
| Money Blues (Armstrong, Hawkins, Redman) | (COL 383D) | 5/19/25 | 20.00 |
| Honeybunch | (GEN 3286) | 3/26/26 | 15.00 |
| When Spring Comes Peeping Through | (GEN 3285) | 3/26/26 | 15.00 |
| The Henderson Stomp (F. Waller, T. Ladnier, Hawkins) | (COL 817D) | 11/03/26 | 25.00 |
| Whiteman Stomp (Waller, Ladnier, Hawkins) | (COL 1002D) | 5/11/27 | 15.00 |
| Old Black Joe's Blues (B. Carter, Hawkins) | (CAM 9003) | 11/28 | 12.00 |
| My Gal Sal (Carter, Kirby, Hawkins) | (COL 2586D) | 2/05/31 | 10.00 |
| Sweet Music | (VIC 22775) | 7/31/31 | 5.00 |
| Strangers | (VIC 22955) | 3/10/32 | 5.00 |
| Poor Old Joe | (VIC 24008) | 3/10/32 | 5.00 |
| New King Porter Stomp | (OKE 41565) | 12/09/32 | 7.50 |
| Nagasaki (vocal "Red" Allen) | (COL 2825D) | 9/22/33 | 5.00 |
| Hocus Pocus | (BLB 5682) | 3/06/34 | 5.00 |
| Limehouse Blues | (DEC 157) | 9/11/34 | 5.00 |
| Down South Camp Meetin' | (DEC 213) | 9/12/34 | 5.00 |
| Rug Cutter's Swing | (DEC 342) | 9/25/34 | 5.00 |
| Christopher Columbus (theme) | (VOC 3211) | 3/27/36 | 5.00 |
| Stealin' Apples | (VOC 3213) | 3/27/36 | 5.00 |
| Riffin' | (VIC 25339) | 5/23/36 | 4.50 |
| Jim Town Blues | (VIC 25379) | 8/04/36 | 4.50 |
| Moten Stomp | (VOC 4180) | 5/28/38 | 4.00 |

*Henderson's records were also made under the names "Dixie Stompers," "Connies Inn Orchestra," and others; and were released on various labels under numerous pseudonyms. See Brian Rust, *Jazz Records, 1917-1942* (1978), vol. 1, 710-729 for a listing.

**HENDERSON, HORACE** and his orchestra

| | | | |
|---|---|---|---|
| Happy Feet | (PHN R-1792) | 10/03/33 | $ 5.00 |
| Rhythm Crazy | (PHN R-1743) | 10/03/33 | 5.00 |
| Ol' Man River | (PHN R-1766) | 10/03/33 | 5.00 |
| Minnie the Moocher's | | | |
| Wedding Day | (PHN R-2031) | 10/03/33 | 5.00 |
| Ain't Cha Glad? | (PHN R-1717) | 10/03/33 | 5.00 |

**HENDERSON, SKITCH**          NMP (.0-.50)

**HERBECK, RAY**          NMP (.0-.25)

**HERMAN, WOODY** and his orchestra
   Generally NMP but for these selections:

| | | | |
|---|---|---|---|
| Wintertime Dreams | (DEC 1056) | 11/06/36 | 4.00 |
| Woodchopper's Ball | (DEC 2440) | 4/12/39 | 3.50 |
| Blues Downstairs/Upstairs | (DEC 2508) | 4/12/39 | 3.00 |
| Blues on Parade | (DEC 2933) | 12/13/39 | 3.00 |
| Golden Wedding | (DEC 3436) | 11/09/40 | 3.00 |
| Blue Flame (theme) | (DEC 3643) | 2/13/41 | 3.50 |
| Bishop's Blues | (DEC 3972) | 8/21/41 | 3.00 |
| Amen | (DEC 18346) | 4/02/42 | 2.50 |
| Apple Honey | (COL 36803) | 2/19/45 | 3.50 |
| Caldonia | (COL 36789) | 2/26/45 | 3.50 |
| Northwest Passage | (COL 36835) | 2/26/45 | 3.50 |
| Bijou | (COL 36861) | 8/20/45 | 3.50 |
| Your Father's Moustache | (COL 36870) | 9/05/45 | 3.00 |
| Wild Root | (COL 36949) | 11/16/45 | 3.00 |
| Ebony Concerto (12", 2 pts.) | (COL 7479M) | 8/19/46 | 4.50 |
| Woodchopper's Ball | (COL 37238) | 12/10/46 | 2.50 |

**HERTH, MILT**          NMP (.0-.25)

**HEYWOOD, EDDIE** and his various groups
   Generally NMP but for these few sides:

| | | | |
|---|---|---|---|
| Begin the Beguine (12") (theme) | (CMD 1514) | 2/19/44 | 4.00 |

**Horace Henderson**     Photograph courtesy Alf Hildman, West Des Moines

**Woody Herman**　　　　　Photograph courtesy Alf Hildman, West Des Moines

| | | | |
|---|---|---|---|
| Them There Eyes (12″) | (SIG 40001) | 3/02/44 | $ 4.00 |
| Night and Day (12″) | | | |
|   (Hodges, Manne) | (SIG 40003) | 5/26/44 | 4.00 |
| Who's Sorry Now? (Bing Crosby) | (DEC 23530) | 9/05/45 | 4.00 |
| The House of Blue Lights | | | |
|   (Andrews Sisters) | (DEC 23641) | 7/27/46 | 2.50 |

**HICKMAN, ART**                     NMP (.0-1.00)

**HIGH HATTERS, THE**               NMP (.0-.50)

**HIGHTOWER'S NIGHTHAWKS**

| | | | |
|---|---|---|---|
| Squeeze Me | (BPT 8045) | 7/20/27 | 30.00 |

**HILDEGARDE**
  Generally NMP except for:

| | | | |
|---|---|---|---|
| Darling, Je Vous Aime Beaucoup | (DEC 23218) | 4/14/41 | 3.00 |

**HILL, TEDDY** and his orchestra

| | | | |
|---|---|---|---|
| Here Comes Cookie | | | |
|   (C. Berry, R. Eldridge) | (BAN 33384) | 2/26/35 | 3.50 |
| When the Robin Sings His | | | |
|   Song Again | (BAN 33397) | 2/26/35 | 3.00 |
| Uptown Rhapsody | (VOC 3294) | 4/01/36 | 2.50 |
| At the Rug Cutter's Ball | (VOC 3247) | 5/04/36 | 2.50 |
| A Study in Brown | (BLB 6943) | 4/23/37 | 3.00 |
| China Boy | (BLB 6941) | 4/23/37 | 3.00 |
| King Porter Stomp (D. Gillespie) | (BLB 6988) | 5/17/37 | 3.00 |
| Blue Rhythm Fantasy (Gillespie) | (BLB 6989) | 5/17/37 | 3.00 |

**HILL, TINY**                       NMP (.0-.75)

**HILO HAWAIIAN ORCHESTRA**      NMP (.0-.10)

**HIMBER, RICHARD**                  NMP (.0-1.00)

**HINES, EARL** and his orchestra

| | | | |
|---|---|---|---|
| Blues in Thirds (piano solo) | (QRS R-7036) | 12/08/28 | 30.00 |
| Chicago High Life (piano solo) | (QRS R-7037) | 12/08/28 | 30.00 |

| | | | |
|---|---|---|---|
| Stowaway | (QRS R-7038) | 12/08/28 | $ 30.00 |
| Panther Rag | (QRS R-7039) | 12/08/28 | 30.00 |
| Caution Blues | (OKE 8832) | 12/09/28 | 15.00 |
| I Ain't Got Nobody | (OKE 8653) | 12/12/28 | 15.00 |
| Sweet Ella May | (VIC 22842) | 2/13/29 | 10.00 |
| Love Me Tonight (piano solo) | (BRN 6403) | 7/14/32 | 10.00 |
| Rosetta | (BRN 6541) | 2/13/33 | 9.00 |
| Pianology | (VOC 3501) | 2/10/37 | 7.50 |
| G.T. Stomp | (BLB 10391) | 7/12/39 | 5.00 |
| Boogie Woogie on St. Louis Blues | (BLB 10674) | 2/13/40 | 4.00 |
| Deep Forest (theme) | (BLB 10727) | 2/13/40 | 3.50 |
| Body and Soul (piano solo) | (BLB 10642) | 2/26/40 | 3.50 |
| The Father Jumps | (BLB 11535) | 10/28/41 | 3.00 |
| The Earl | (BLB 11432) | 11/17/41 | 3.00 |
| Second Balcony Jump | (BLB 11567) | 3/19/42 | 3.00 |
| Squeeze Me | (SIG 28109) | 2/26/44 | 3.00 |
| Life with Fatha | (APO 356) | 4/26/44 | 3.00 |

**HITE, LES** and his orchestra
   Generally NMP but for the classic:

| | | | |
|---|---|---|---|
| The World Is Waiting for the Sunrise | (BLB 11109) | 3/06/41 | 3.00 |

**HODGES, JOHNNY** and his orchestra

| | | | |
|---|---|---|---|
| Foolin' Myself (Ellington, Bigard, Carney) | (VAY 576) | 5/20/37 | 6.00 |
| Sailboat in the Moonlight (Buddy Clark) | (VAY 586) | 5/20/37 | 6.00 |
| Jeep's Blues | (VOC 4115) | 3/28/38 | 5.00 |
| Empty Ballroom Blues | (VOC 4213) | 6/22/38 | 4.00 |
| Jitterbug's Lullaby | (VOC 4309) | 8/01/38 | 3.50 |
| Day Dream | (BLB 11021) | 11/02/40 | 3.50 |
| Thing's Ain't What They Used to Be | (BLB 11447) | 7/03/41 | 3.50 |

**HOFF, CARL**                    NMP (.0-.25)

**Les Hite**  Photograph courtesy Alf Hildman, West Des Moines

## HOLIDAY, BILLIE
and her orchestra, vocals

| | | | TIP |
|---|---|---|---|
| Did I Remember? (A. Shaw, Berigan, Bushkin) | (VOC 3276) | 7/10/36 | $ 6.00 |
| Billie's Blues | (VOC 3288) | 7/10/36 | 6.00 |
| A Fine Romance | (VOC 3333) | 9/29/36 | 5.00 |
| Got My Love to Keep Me Warm (T. Wilson, J. Kirby) | (VOC 3431) | 1/12/37 | 5.00 |
| Me, Myself and I (E. Hall, L. Young, W. Page) | (VOC 3593) | 6/15/37 | 5.00 |
| He's Funny That Way (Thornhill) | (VOC 3748) | 9/13/37 | 5.00 |
| On the Sentimental Side (T. Wilson) | (VOC 3947) | 1/12/38 | 5.00 |
| Dream of Life (Shavers, C. Berry, C. Cole) | (VOC 4631) | 1/20/39 | 4.00 |
| Strange Fruit | (CMD 526) | 4/20/39 | 5.00 |
| Yesterdays | (CMD 527) | 4/20/39 | 4.00 |
| Them There Eyes | (VOC 5021) | 7/05/39 | 3.50 |
| The Man I Love | (VOC 5377) | 12/13/39 | 4.00 |
| Body and Soul (Roy Eldridge) | (VOC 5481) | 2/29/40 | 4.00 |
| I Hear Music (Eldridge, Redman, Auld, Byas) | (OKE 5831) | 9/12/40 | 4.00 |
| St. Louis Blues (B. Carter) | (OKE 6064) | 10/15/40 | 5.00 |
| Georgia on My Mind (E. Heywood) | (OKE 6134) | 3/21/41 | 4.00 |
| Love Me or Leave Me | (OKE 6369) | 8/07/41 | 3.50 |
| It's a Sin to Tell a Lie | (HAR 1075) | 2/10/42 | 3.50 |
| Lover Man | (DEC 23391) | 10/04/44 | 3.50 |
| Good Morning Heartache | (DEC 23676) | 1/22/46 | 3.50 |
| Baby, I Don't Cry Over You | (DEC 23957) | 4/09/46 | 3.50 |
| Solitude | (DEC 23853) | 2/13/47 | 3.50 |

## HOLMAN, LIBBY
Generally NMP but for a few sentimental items:

| | | | |
|---|---|---|---|
| Moanin' Low | (BRN 4445) | 7/29 | 5.50 |
| Why Was I Born? | (BRN 4570) | 11/29 | 4.00 |

**Lena Horne**

Photograph courtesy RCA Victor

| | | | |
|---|---|---|---|
| More Than You Know | (BRN 4613) | 12/29 | $ 4.00 |
| Body and Soul | (BRN 4910) | 10/30 | 4.00 |
| Love for Sale | (BRN 6045) | 1/31 | 3.50 |
| You and the Night and the Music | | | |
| (R. Himber) | (VIC 24839) | 12/19/34 | 3.00 |

**HOPKINS, CLAUDE** and his orchestra

| | | | |
|---|---|---|---|
| Mad Moments | (COL 2665D) | 5/24/32 | 6.00 |
| Mush Mouth | (COL 2674D) | 5/24/32 | 6.00 |
| Canadian Capers | (COL 2747D) | 1/13/33 | 5.00 |
| California, Here I Come | (COL 2741D) | 1/13/33 | 5.00 |
| Washington Squabble | (BRN 6750) | 12/11/33 | 5.00 |
| Harlem Rhythm Dance | (COL 2880D) | 1/11/34 | 4.00 |
| Minor Mania | (COL 2904D) | 1/11/34 | 4.00 |
| Three Little Words | (BRN 6864) | 4/06/34 | 4.00 |
| Margie | (BRN 6916) | 5/03/34 | 3.50 |
| King Porter Stomp | (DEC 184) | 9/14/34 | 4.00 |

**HORLICK, HARRY**                NMP (.0-.10)

**HORNE, LENA**
Generally NMP with these few exceptions:

| | | | |
|---|---|---|---|
| That's What Love Did to Me | | | |
| (Noble Sissle) | (DEC 778) | 3/11/36 | 5.00 |
| St. Louis Blues | (VIC 27542) | 6/23/41 | 3.50 |
| Aunt Hagar's Blues | (VIC 27544) | 6/25/41 | 3.50 |
| Don't Take Your Love from Me | | | |
| (A. Shaw) | (VIC 27509) | 6/26/41 | 3.50 |
| Out of Nowhere (T. Wilson) | (COL 26737) | 9/16/41 | 3.50 |
| Stormy Weather | (VIC 27819) | 12/15/41 | 3.00 |
| The Man I Love | (VIC 27818) | 12/15/41 | 3.00 |
| Moanin' Love | (VIC 27817) | 12/17/41 | 3.00 |

**HOWARD, EDDY**                NMP (.0-1.00)

**HUDSON-DE LANGE ORCHESTRA**

| | | | |
|---|---|---|---|
| Tormented | (BRN 7598) | 1/15/36 | 5.00 |

| | | | |
|---|---|---|---|
| Eight Bars in Search of a Melody (theme) | (BRN 7618) | 1/15/36 | $ 5.50 |
| Organ Grinder's Swing | (BRN 7656) | 3/20/36 | 4.00 |
| Monopoly Swing | (BRN 7667) | 3/20/36 | 4.00 |
| I Never Knew | (BRN 7708) | 6/20/36 | 4.00 |
| Mr. Ghost Goes to Town | (BRN 7715) | 6/20/36 | 3.50 |
| Cross Country Hop | (BRN 7743) | 8/13/36 | 3.00 |
| Midnight at the Onyx | (BRN 7795) | 11/23/36 | 3.00 |
| If I Could Be with You | (BRN 8016) | 5/27/37 | 3.00 |
| Goin' Haywire | (BRN 8007) | 8/20/37 | 2.50 |
| China Clipper | (BRN 8147) | 4/08/38 | 2.50 |
| On the Alamo | (BRN 8156) | 4/08/38 | 2.50 |

**HUDSON, DEAN**  NMP (.0-.25)

**HUTTON, BETTY**  NMP (.0-.50)

**HUTTON, INA RAY** and her orchestras
Generally NMP but for these few sides:

| | | | |
|---|---|---|---|
| How's About Tomorrow Night? (all female orch.) | (VIC 24692) | 7/12/34 | 5.00 |
| Wild Party (all female) | (VOC 2816) | 9/13/34 | 4.00 |
| Twenty-Four Hours in Georgia (all female) | (VOC 2801) | 9/13/34 | 4.00 |

**HYLTON, JACK**  NMP (.0-1.00)

# I

**INK SPOTS, THE**
Generally NMP with these possible exceptions:

| | | | |
|---|---|---|---|
| Your Feet's Too Big | (VIC 24851) | 1/04/35 | 5.00 |
| Swing, Gate, Swing | (VIC 24876) | 1/04/35 | 5.00 |
| If I Didn't Care | (DEC 2286) | 1/12/39 | 2.50 |
| Maybe | (DEC 3258) | 6/11/40 | 2.50 |
| We Three | (DEC 3379) | 7/16/40 | 2.50 |
| Java Jive | (DEC 3432) | 7/16/40 | 2.50 |

**Four Ink Spots**  Photograph courtesy Alf Hildman, West Des Moines

## INTERNATIONAL NOVELTY
## ORCHESTRA                                   NMP (.0-.20)

## IPANA TROUBADOURS

Paddlin' Madelin' Home
(R. Nichols)              (COL 503D)    10/30/25   $ 7.50
Nagasaki                  (COL 1463D)    6/29/28     6.00
Glorianna
(T. Dorsey, B. Goodman)   (COL 1638D)   10/25/28     7.50
I'll Get By (Bing Crosby) (COL 1694D)   12/28/28     8.00

# J

## JAMES, BILLY                                 NMP (.0-.50)

## JAMES, HARRY and his orchestra

I Can Dream Can't I?
(Stacy, W. Page)             (BRN 8038)   12/01/37   6.00
Life Goes to a Party         (BRN 8035)   12/01/37   4.00
One O'clock Jump             (BRN 8055)    1/05/38   4.00
Ciribiribin (theme)          (BRN 8327)    2/20/39   3.00
Two O'clock Jump             (BRN 8337)    3/06/39   3.00
King Porter Stomp            (BRN 8366)    4/06/39   3.00
Melancholy Mood (F. Sinatra) (BRN 8443)    7/13/39   3.00
My Buddy (Sinatra)           (COL 35242)   8/17/39   4.00
All or Nothing at All (Sinatra) (COL 35587) 8/31/39  4.00
On a Little Street in Singapore
(Sinatra)                    (COL 35261)  10/13/39   4.00
Flash                        (COL 35587)  11/08/39   3.50
Ciribiribin (Sinatra)        (COL 35316)  11/08/39   3.50
Concerto for Trumpet         (COL 35340)  11/30/39   3.00
Night Special                (COL 35456)  11/30/39   3.00
Flight of the Bumble Bee     (VAR 8298)      5/40    3.50
Music Makers                 (COL 35932)   1/08/41   3.00
Trumpet Rhapsody (2 pts.)    (COL 36160)     3/26,
                                             4/28/41  3.00

**Harry James**          Photograph courtesy Alf Hildman, West Des Moines

| | | | |
|---|---|---|---|
| I'll Get By (Dick Haymes) | (COL 36285) | 4/07/41 | $ 3.00 |
| You Made Me Love You | (COL 36296) | 5/20/41 | 3.00 |
| The Mole | (COL 36599) | 11/30/41 | 2.50 |
| Strictly Instrumental | (COL 36579) | 11/30/41 | 2.50 |
| Sleepy Lagoon | (COL 36549) | 2/24/42 | 2.75 |
| Crazy Rhythm | (COL 36545) | 2/24/42 | 2.50 |
| Prince Charming | (COL 36672) | 7/22/42 | 2.50 |
| I've Heard That Song Before | (COL 36668) | 7/31/42 | 2.75 |
| I'm Beginning to See the Light | (COL 36758) | 11/21/44 | 2.50 |
| When Your Lover Has Gone | (COL 36773) | 11/21/44 | 2.50 |
| Carnival | (COL 36827) | 2/14/45 | 2.50 |
| 9:20 Special | (COL 36887) | 5/30/45 | 2.50 |
| I Can't Begin to Tell You (Betty Grable) | (COL 36867) | 8/20/45 | 3.00 |
| The Beaumont Ride | (COL 37080) | 12/19/45 | 2.50 |
| Easy | (COL 36996) | 5/22/46 | 2.00 |

**JARRETT, ART**                    NMP (.0-.50)

**JENNEY, JACK**                    NMP (.0-.75)

**JESSEL, GEORGE**

| | | | |
|---|---|---|---|
| My Mother's Eyes | (VIC 21852) | 1/18/29 | 4.00 |
| Hello, Momma (2 pts.) | (DEC 1484) | 9/10/37 | 3.00 |

**JOHNSON, JOHNNY**                 NMP (.0-.75)

**JOHNSTON, JOHNNIE**               NMP (.0-.50)

**JOLSON, AL**
 Generally NMP excepting:

| | | | |
|---|---|---|---|
| That Haunting Melody | (VIC 17037) | 12/22/11 | 25.00 |
| Rock-a-Bye Your Baby | (COL A-2560) | 3/13/18 | 10.00 |
| Swanee | (COL A-2884) | 1/09/20 | 10.00 |
| Avalon | (COL A-2995) | 8/16/20 | 8.00 |
| April Showers | (COL A-3500) | 10/22/21 | 8.00 |
| Toot, Toot, Tootsie | (COL A-3705) | 9/11/22 | 8.00 |
| California, Here I Come | (BRN 2569) | 3/24 | 7.50 |
| Back in Your Own Backyard | (BRN 3867) | 1/28 | 7.00 |

| There's a Rainbow 'Round My Shoulder | (BRN 4033) | 8/20/28 | $ 10.00 |
|---|---|---|---|

**JONES, ALLAN**          NMP (.0-.50)

**JONES, ISHAM**          NMP (.0-1.25)

**JONES, SPIKE** and His City Slickers          TIP

| | | | |
|---|---|---|---|
| Red Wing | (BLB 11282) | 8/08/41 | 2.50 |
| Pass the Biscuits, Mirandy | (BLB 11530) | 4/07/42 | 2.50 |
| Hotchia Cornia | (BLB 30-0818) | 7/28/42 | 2.50 |
| Der Fuehrer's Face | (BLB 11586) | 7/28/42 | 3.50 |
| Oh! By Jingo | (BLB 30-0812) | 7/28/42 | 2.50 |

**JORDAN, LOUIS** and his Tympany Five
Generally NMP but for these:

| | | | |
|---|---|---|---|
| Is You Is Or Is You Ain't My Baby? | (DEC 8659) | 10/04/43 | 2.75 |
| My Baby Said Yes (Bing Crosby) | (DEC 23417) | 7/26/44 | 5.00 |
| Stone Cold Dead in the Market (E. Fitzgerald) | (DEC 23546) | 10/09/45 | 3.00 |

**JOY, JIMMY**          NMP (.0-.50)

**JOY, LEONARD**          NMP (.0-.25)

**JURGENS, DICK**          NMP (.0-1.25)

# K

**KAHN, ART**          NMP (.0-.25)

**KAHN, ROGER WOLFE** and his orchestra
Generally NMP with these modest exceptions:

| | | | |
|---|---|---|---|
| Let a Smile Be Your Umbrella (M. Mole, Venuti) | (VIC 21233) | 2/8/28 | 3.00 |
| She's a Great, Great Girl (J. Teagarden) | (VIC 21326) | 3/14/28 | 3.00 |
| Pretty Little Thing (J. Dorsey, Venuti, B. Russin) | (BRN 4374) | 5/15/29 | 3.00 |

| | | | |
|---|---|---|---|
| When a Woman Loves a Man (Libby Holman) | (BRN 4699) | 1/22/30 | $ 3.00 |
| My Silent Love (A. Shaw) | (COL 2653D) | 5/04/32 | 3.00 |

**KARDOS, GENE**  NMP (.0-.50)

**KASSEL, ART**  NMP (.0-.75)

**KATZ, AL**  NMP (.0-.25)

**KAVELIN, AL**  NMP (.0-.50)

**KAY, BEATRICE**  NMP (.0-.25)

**KAY, HERBIE**  NMP (.0-.50)

**KAYE, DANNY**  NMP (.0-1.00)

**KAYE, SAMMY**  NMP (.0-1.00)

**KEMP, HAL\*** and his orchestra
Generally NMP but for these recordings:

| | | | |
|---|---|---|---|
| Bye Bye Baby (as Carolina Club Orch.) | (PAT 036181) | 11/19/24 | 10.00 |
| Blue Rhythm | (COL 671D) | 4/20/26 | 5.00 |
| Mary Ann (Hal Kemp assists vocal) | (BRN 3792) | 1/25/28 | 5.00 |
| Washington and Lee Swing | (BRN 4078) | 9/28/28 | 5.00 |
| Washin' the Blues from My Soul (B. Berigan) | (BRN 4805) | 5/09/30 | 5.00 |
| Medley of Southern College Songs (2 pts.) | (BRN 4958) | 10/17/30 | 5.00 |
| Shuffle Off to Buffalo | (BRN 6471) | 12/32 | 4.00 |
| A Heart of Stone | (BRN 6574) | 5/04/33 | 4.00 |
| Whispers in the Dark | (VIC 25598) | 6/01/37 | 3.50 |
| Got a Date with an Angel (theme) | (VIC 25651) | 7/22/37 | 3.50 |
| A Heart of Stone | (VIC 26165) | 1/26/39 | 3.00 |
| Love for Sale | (VIC 26278) | 5/19/39 | 3.00 |
| The Breeze and I (Janet Blair) | (VIC 26615) | 5/11/40 | 2.50 |

\*Kemp's band also recorded for HAR, BAN, OKE as the Carolina Collegians and Hal's Dixie Collegians (1924-32). Range: $4-5.00.

**Art Kassel**　　　　　Photograph courtesy Alf Hildman, West Des Moines

**Ray Michaels with Sammy Kay and his orchestra**
Photograph courtesy Val Air Ballroom, West Des Moines

**Pnina with Sammy Kay and his orchestra**
Photograph courtesy Val Air Ballroom, West Des Moines

# INTERMISSION 4

## *The Big Four Revisited*

To those among us who were dependent upon 78's for entertainment the terms "Columbia," "Victor," "Decca," and "Capitol" conveyed a special message. There were scores of other labels of course, but between 1925 and 1945 the big four dominated our imaginations (and the marketplace). Very few of us know much about the historical derivations or corporate intricacies of the companies we spoke of so glibly. That did not matter a great deal at the time. What counted were the music, the bands, the vocalists and sidemen, anticipating new releases, and collecting favored discs. I, for one, was totally oblivious to anything more sophisticated than the letters on the labels. If someone had asked: "Say, I wonder how these records got their trade names?" — I would have had to confess my absolute ignorance.

To save you the time it might take to exhume the facts, and to whet your appetite to investigate even further, I offer these abridged profiles of the big four. I think you will find these mini-histories interesting, perhaps surprising. At least you will feel a bit more knowledgeable about those labels you see at garage sales and flea markets. Now all you have to do is wait for someone to come along and inquire: "Say, do you know how these 'Victor' records got their name?" — and you can swing into action.

### COLUMBIA

The saga of Columbia records is intricate and compelling. Mythology aside, Columbia is not the oldest disc-producing company in the U.S.A. Founded by Edward Easton (1888) the Columbia Phonograph Company trafficked in cylinders (1888-1912) and discs from 1902. Columbia pioneered the two-sided record (1908), furniture-like consoles, and signed some of the best classical artists of the 1904-1920 period. The colorful, beribboned, red-white-blue Columbia labels from that era still proliferate wherever old records are stored. Even though gross sales reached $45 million in 1919 a postwar recession forced Columbia to divest itself of its British (1922) and Dictaphone holdings (1923). Deprived by death (1915) of Edward Easton's wisdom, the company lapsed into receivership in 1923. Louis Sterling of British Columbia purchased the sagging company and a revival began (1926-30), due largely to new recording methods. (Note the words "electrical process" on the black label Columbias released in the late 1920s.) Sold off again in 1931 Columbia limped through the Depression until it was bought up (along with Brunswick, Vocalion, Perfect, and Melotone) for $70,500 by the American Record Company in 1934. In December, 1938, the Columbia Broadcasting Company (which, ironically, had gotten its name from the Columbia Phonograph Company in 1927) purchased the drifting company for $800,000. The first red label 10″ Columbia discs we loved so well for two decades were released in the fateful summer of 1939. A stable of popular bands (Goodman, Kyser, Heidt, O. Tucker, James, *et al)* and a solid line of low-priced classical discs vaulted Columbia into second place among the big four by 1941. This sturdy CBS division survived the 1942-44 record ban, introduced the LP (1948), and popularized the mail-order record club (1955). In 1977 Columbia Records brought to the CBS enterprise $768 million in revenues. Hail, Columbia!

## *VICTOR*

The disc-producing Victor Talking Machine Company was incorporated in October, 1901, the brainchild of Eldridge Johnson. Within two years Victor had attained profits of $1 million, published its initial catalog, and cut its first "Red Seal" record. For the next twenty years Victor enjoyed a remarkable string of achievements. It signed Enrico Caruso (1904); developed the "Victrola" (1906); perfected the recording arts and sciences; issued the *Victor Book of the Opera* (1912); led the industry in advertising techniques; diversified successfully into popular music and jazz (1916-18); and, in the process, increased its assets from $3 million to $51 million (1921). A slack period (1922-25) was relieved by the adoption of the new electrical recording system, a roster of recognized musicians (Whiteman, Vallee, Weems, Olson, Waring, Goldkette, etc.), and a resurgence of public interest in radio-phonographs. In

December, 1926, Johnson sold his 245,000 shares to a Wall Street group for $22 million. The Radio Corporation of America (founded 1919) bought out the bankers (January, 1929) and the Victor Talking Machine Company became the RCA Victor division of the parent company. Hit hard by the Depression, Victor was resuscitated by creative leadership and experienced an upswing in 1934-36. With bands such as Goodman, T. Dorsey, Shaw, and Miller under contract, Victor monopolized the pop record market until 1940 (when Columbia and Decca began to assert themselves). Victor staggered through the record ban (1942-44), returned to prominence in the industry (1946-48), and unleashed the 45 rpm on the public in 1949. When RCA bought Elvis Presley from Sun Records for $35,000 in 1955 the future solvency of Victor Records was assured. RCA, CBS, and Warner corner more than 70 percent of all revenues from recordings each year. Thank you, Eldridge Johnson (1867-1945).

## DECCA

If you saw the Errol Flynn film *Dawn Patrol* (1938) you will recall that the tune "Poor Butterfly" was featured throughout. Chances are that primitive, portable phonograph the RFC officers used was invented by Samuel Barnett and carried the tradename "Decca." The Decca machine was employed widely by British troops during WWI. The Decca Record Company was formed in London (1929) and was headed by stockbroker E. R. (Sir Ted) Lewis. (My guess is that the word Decca was derived from the Deccan plateau in India, then under British supervision.) American Decca was incorporated on August 4, 1934, by Jack Kapp, an experienced Chicago-born record entrepreneur, who visited Lewis in 1933 and returned to the U.S.A. with domestic rights to the Decca line. In August-September, 1934, Bing Crosby, the Mills Brothers, Guy Lombardo (who defected to Victor for three years, 1935-38), Casa Loma, and the battling Dorsey Brothers cut sides for Kapp and the blue-gold Decca label made its debut. There were other low-budget records (Bluebird, Okeh, Vocalion) but none offered the caliber of performer Decca did at thirty-five cents apiece. By 1938 Decca's profits exceeded $300,000. Decca and Victor accounted for 75 percent of the 33 million discs sold that (pre-Columbian) year. The company's fortunes rose steadily until the record ban, reaching the $1 million profit level in 1942, and Kapp avoided disaster by capitulating to the American Federation of Musicians (AFM) in September, 1943. Shortly thereafter Decca's original cast album of *Oklahoma!* sold 1.3 million copies (at $5 per unit). By then Decca had converted to the black-gold label. Jack Kapp died the year Decca switched from 78's to LP (1949). Decca merged with Universal pictures (1952) and was taken over by the Music Corporation of America (MCA) a decade later. Thirty years after Kapp's untimely passing the Decca label is defunct but its lineal descendant MCA Records is worth nearly $100 million in yearly revenues. Hats off to the house that Jack built.

## CAPITOL

The Depression hit the British recording industry hard in 1930-31. One outcome was the merger of two rival groups, HMV and Columbia, into the Electrical and Musical Industries, Ltd. (EMI) in 1931. More about that below. Eleven years later in Los Angeles songwriters Johnny Mercer and George G. (Buddy) De Sylva and businessman Glenn Wallichs combined resources to form Capitol Records (after they toyed with the idea of naming it "Liberty" records) in April, 1942. Their first black-silver label discs were cut that month by Paul Whiteman. Despite the record ban Capitol grossed $195,000 by October, 1942, an auspicious beginning by any standard. One year thereafter Capitol signed with the AFM and began to produce records in earnest. With performers such as Jo Stafford, the Pied Pipers, Nat Cole, Stan Kenton, and Mercer himself Capitol could hardly have failed. Within five years of its inception Capitol had earned unqualified admission to the inner circle: the Big Three became the Big Four. A $14.5 million gross (1947) and active sales branches in twenty-nine cities made Capitol a true competitor to the older companies. In 1949 Capitol was producing discs at 78, 45, and 33⅓ speeds. The roster of stars grew: Billy May, Ray Anthony, Les Paul and Mary Ford, Dean Martin, Kay Starr, Peggy Lee — and, a real coup, Frank Sinatra joined the purple label gang in 1953. Suddenly, in 1955, the change came. Seven years earlier the Wallichs-De Sylva-Mercer group dissolved itself and stocks were issued to public buyers.

Capitol was bought out in 1955 by EMI (71 percent) for $8.5 million and the close-knit company was led into international waters, never to be quite the same again. A decade later the Beatles catapulted Capitol-EMI into the higher brackets once more. By 1970 gross sales hit $178 million. Wallichs, De Sylva, and Mercer are gone, but the melody lingers on.

In truth, the Big Four dominated the recording industry for a scant dozen years (1942-1954), although it seems a lot longer. Their trade names are burned into our imaginations so deeply that we overlook the mutations of the past twenty-five years in a stubborn attempt to preserve our memories of simpler times when companies were personal — and labels came in just a few basic colors. Ah, the good old days.

Sources for further reading: Steve Chapple and Reebe Garofalo, *Rock 'n' Roll Is Here to Pay* (Nelson-Hall, 1977); Dave Dexter, Jr., "Playback" *(Billboard,* 1976); "The Gorillas Are Coming," *Forbes* (July 10, 1978); Gelatt, *The Fabulous Phonograph,* op cit.; Robert Metz, *CBS: Reflections in a Bloodshot Eye* (Signet; New York; 1976); New York *Times* (March 26, 1949) 17; "Who Owns the Media," *Take One* (November, 1978), 24, 26-28, 58-59; E.R. Fenimore Johnson, *His Master's Voice Was Eldridge R. Johnson* (Privately printed; Milford, Delaware; 1974); Read and Welch, *Tin Foil to Stereo, op cit.*

**Hal Kemp**  Photograph courtesy Alf Hildman, West Des Moines

To "alf"
With sincere good wishes —
Janet Blair

**Janet Blair featured with Hal Kemp**

Photograph courtesy Alf Hildman, West Des Moines

**Bob Allen featured with Hal Kemp**

Photograph courtesy Alf Hildman, West Des Moines

**KENDIS, SONNY**                    NMP (.0-.25)

**KENTON, STAN** and his orchestra

| | | | |
|---|---|---|---|
| The Nango | (DEC 4037) | 9/11/41 | $ 6.00 |
| Adios | (DEC 4038) | 9/11/41 | 5.00 |
| Concerto for Doghouse | (DEC 4254) | 2/13/42 | 4.00 |
| El Choclo | (DEC 4319) | 2/13/42 | 4.00 |
| Gambler's Blues (12″) | (DEC 15063) | 2/13/42 | 6.00 |
| Artistry in Rhythm (theme) | (CAP 159) | 11/19/43 | 3.00 |
| Balboa Bash | (CAP 10040) | 11/15/44 | 2.50 |
| Tampico | (CAP 202) | 5/04/45 | 2.50 |
| Painted Rhythm | (CAP 250) | 10/03/45 | 2.50 |
| Concerto to End All Concertos | | | |
| (2 pts.) | (CAP 382) | 7/46 | 3.00 |
| Unison Riff | (CAP 15018) | 10/22/47 | 2.50 |

**KEPPARD, FREDDIE** and his Jazz Cardinals

| | | | |
|---|---|---|---|
| Stock Yards Strut | (PAR 12399) | 9/26 | 50.00 |

**KING, HENRY**                      NMP (.0-.25)

**KING, WAYNE** and his orchestra
  Generally NMP but for:

| | | | |
|---|---|---|---|
| The Waltz You Saved for Me | | | |
| (theme) | (VIC 22575) | 11/07/30 | 3.50 |
| Time Was (Buddy Clark vocal) | (VIC 27535) | 6/21/41 | 3.00 |

**KIRBY, JOHN** and his various groups

| | | | |
|---|---|---|---|
| Pastel Blue (C. Shavers, B. Kyle) | (DEC 2367) | 10/28/38 | 3.50 |
| Undecided | (DEC 2216) | 10/28/38 | 3.00 |
| Effervescent Blues | (VOC 4624) | 1/09/39 | 3.00 |
| Anitra's Dance | (VOC 4890) | 5/19/39 | 3.00 |
| Royal Garden Blues | (VOC 5187) | 7/28/39 | 3.00 |
| Nocturne | (VOC 5520) | 10/12/39 | 3.00 |
| Jumpin' in the Pump Room | (OKE 5661) | 4/22/40 | 2.50 |
| Blues Petite | (OKE 5805) | 5/27/40 | 2.50 |
| It's Only a Paper Moon | (VIC 27598) | 7/25/41 | 2.50 |
| St. Louis Blues | (VIC 27926) | 2/11/42 | 3.00 |

**Wayne King**
Photograph courtesy Alf Hildman, West Des Moines

**KIRK, ANDY** and his Clouds of Joy
  Generally NMP except these possibilities:

| | | | |
|---|---|---|---|
| Mess-a-Stomp | (BRN 4694) | 11/07/29 | $ 5.00 |
| Cloudy | (BRN 4653) | 11/07/29 | 5.00 |
| Lotta Sax Appeal | (DEC 1046) | 3/02/36 | 3.50 |
| Moten Swing | (DEC 853) | 3/02/36 | 3.50 |
| Big Jim Blues | (DEC 2915) | 11/15/39 | 3.00 |
| The Count | (DEC 18123) | 11/07/40 | 2.50 |

**KLEIN, MANNIE** and his orchestra

| | | | |
|---|---|---|---|
| Hot Spell (B. Wain, A. Shaw, J. Jenney) | (BRN 7606) | 1/20/36 | 4.00 |

**KNAPP, ORVILLE**          NMP (.0-1.00)

**KORN KOBBLERS**          NMP (.0-.20)

**KRUPA, GENE** and his various groups

| | | | |
|---|---|---|---|
| Jazz Me Blues (Goodman, Stacy) | (PHN R-2268) | 11/19/35 | 7.50 |
| Three Little Words | (PHN R-2224) | 11/19/35 | 7.50 |
| Swing Is Here (Goodman, C. Berry, Eldridge) | (VIC 25276) | 2/29/36 | 6.00 |
| Mutiny in the Parlor | (VIC 25263) | 2/29/36 | 6.00 |
| Grandfather's Clock | (BRN 8124) | 4/14/38 | 5.00 |
| Wire Brush Stomp | (BRN 8166) | 6/02/38 | 5.00 |
| Bolero at the Savoy (Irene Daye) | (BRN 8284) | 12/01/38 | 4.00 |
| Symphony in Riffs | (COL 35387) | 9/20/39 | 3.50 |
| Drummin' Man | (COL 35324) | 11/02/39 | 3.50 |
| Blue Rhythm Fantasy (2 pts.) | (OKE 5627) | 1/02/40 | 4.00 |
| Rhumboogie | (OKE 5788) | 9/03/40 | 3.50 |
| Drum Boogie | (OKE 6046) | 1/17/41 | 3.50 |
| After You've Gone (R. Eldridge) | (OKE 6278) | 6/05/41 | 3.50 |
| Thanks for the Boogie Ride | (OKE 6506) | 11/25/41 | 3.50 |
| Leave Us Leap | (COL 36802) | 1/22/45 | 2.50 |
| What's This? | (COL 36819) | 1/22/45 | 2.50 |
| Opus No. 1 | (COL 37224) | 8/21/45 | 2.50 |
| Lover | (COL 36986) | 10/23/45 | 2.50 |
| Disc Jockey Jump | (COL 37589) | 1/22/47 | 2.50 |

**Harry Babbitt vocalist featured with Kay Kyser**
Photograph courtesy Alf Hildman, West Des Moines

**KUHN, DICK**                             NMP (.0-.20)

**KYSER, KAY** and his orchestra
  Generally NMP with a few exceptions:

| | | | |
|---|---|---|---|
| Broken Dreams of Yesterday | (VIC V-40028) | 11/26/28 | $ 8.00 |
| Collegiate Fanny | (VIC V-40258) | 11/26/29 | 7.50 |
| Rainy Weather | (VIC V-40222) | 11/26/29 | 7.50 |
| Take Your Girlie to the Movies | (BRN 7453) | 5/09/35 | 4.00 |

# L

**LAMOUR, DOROTHY**                    NMP (.0-1.00)

**LANDRY, ART** and his Call of the North Orchestra

| | | | |
|---|---|---|---|
| Secrets | (GEN 5053) | 2/12/23 | 10.00 |
| Dreamy Melody | (GEN 5255) | 2/12/23 | 10.00 |
| Barcarolle | (GEN 5170) | 6/01/23 | 7.50 |
| Some of These Days | (GEN 5189) | 6/15/23 | 7.50 |
| Rip Saw Blues | (GEN 5171) | 6/15/23 | 7.50 |
| Choo Choo Blues | | | |
| (Syncopatin' Six) | (GEN 5184) | 6/16/23 | 7.00 |
| Poppies | (GEN 5222) | 7/13/23 | 6.50 |

**LANGFORD, FRANCES**                  NMP (.0-.50)

**LANIN, SAM**                         NMP (.0-1.00)

**LAVAL, PAUL**                        NMP (.0-1.00)

**LAWRENCE, GERTRUDE**

| | | | |
|---|---|---|---|
| A Cup of Coffee . . . | | | |
| (Jack Buchanan) | (COL 512D) | 11/17/25 | 10.00 |
| Poor Little Rich Girl | (COL 513D) | 11/17/25 | 8.00 |
| Russian Blues | (COL 514D) | 11/17/25 | 7.50 |
| Do-Do-Do | (VIC 20331) | 10/29/26 | 7.50 |
| This Is New | (VIC 27331) | 2/23/41 | 3.50 |
| My Ship | (VIC 27330) | 2/23/41 | 3.50 |

**LEVINE, HENRY**                      NMP (.0-.75)

**Sully Mason soloist featured with Kay Kyser**

Photograph courtesy Alf Hildman, West Des Moines

**LEWIS, TED** and his various groups
Generally NMP but for the following:

| | | | |
|---|---|---|---|
| Blues My Naughty Sweetie Taught to Me | (COL A-2798) | 9/05/19 | $ 8.00 |
| When My Baby Smiles at Me (theme) | (COL 922D) | 11/22/26 | 5.00 |
| Some of These Days (Sophie Tucker) | (COL 826D) | 11/23/26 | 5.50 |
| Clarinet Marmalade | (COL 1573D) | 7/16/28 | 4.00 |
| Medicine Man for the Blues (Spanier, Brunies) | (COL 1882D) | 5/26/29 | 4.00 |
| Farewell Blues (F. Teschmacher) | (COL 2029D) | 8/21/29 | 4.00 |
| At Last I'm Happy (Goodman, Spanier) | (COL 2408) | 1/12/31 | 4.00 |
| Dallas Blues (Waller, Goodman, Spanier) | (COL 2428D) | 3/06/31 | 4.50 |
| When My Baby Smiles at Me (theme) | (DEC 2054) | 7/16/38 | 3.00 |

**LIGHT, ENOCH**                 NMP (.0-.50)

**LITTLE, LITTLE JACK**          NMP (.0-.25)

**LOGAN, ELLA**                  NMP (.0-.25)

**LOMBARDO, GUY**
Generally NMP but for these few exceptions:

| | | | |
|---|---|---|---|
| Cotton Picker's Ball | (GEN 5417) | 3/10/24 | 15.00 |
| So This Is Venice | (GEN 5416) | 3/10/24 | 15.00 |
| Too Late (Kate Smith vocal) | (COL 2578D) | 12/08/31 | 5.00 |
| You Are Too Beautiful (Al Jolson) | (BRN 6500) | 12/20/32 | 10.00 |
| April Showers (Jolson) | (BRN 6502) | 12/20/32 | 10.00 |
| You're Getting to Be a Habit ... (Bing Crosby) | (BRN 6472) | 1/12/33 | 10.00 |
| You're Beautiful Tonight ... (B. Crosby) | (BRN 6477) | 1/12/33 | 10.00 |
| Boo-Hoo | (VIC 25522) | 2/02/37 | 4.00 |
| Auld Lang Syne (theme) | (DEC 2478) | 3/07/39 | 3.50 |

**Ted Lewis**  Photograph courtesy Alf Hildman, West Des Moines

**Guy Lombardo**
Photograph courtesy Alf Hildman,
West Des Moines

WALTZES

*played by*
**GUY LOMBARDO**
and his royal canadians

DECCA RECORDS

**LONG, JOHNNY**                                  NMP (.0-.75)

**LOPEZ, VINCENT** and his orchestra
  Generally NMP but for this modest group:

| | | | |
|---|---|---|---|
| Bluin' the Blues | (EDI 50662) | 1/09/20 | $ 5.00 |
| The Sheik of Araby | (BSW 2043) | 12/21 | 8.00 |
| Nola (theme) | (OKE 4579) | 3/20/22 | 4.00 |
| Just a Memory | | | |
|   (J. Dorsey, X. Cugat) | (BRN 3633) | 8/22/27 | 3.50 |
| The Jitterbug (Betty Hutton vocal) | (BLB 10367) | 7/05/39 | 4.00 |
| Nola | (BLB 10601) | 1/08/40 | 3.00 |

**LORCH, CARL**                                  NMP (.0-.25)

**LOWN, BERT** and his various groups
  Generally NMP excepting the following:

| | | | |
|---|---|---|---|
| Big City Blues (Miff Mole) | (HAR 920-H) | 4/05/29 | 4.00 |
| Jazz Me Blues (Mole) | (HAR 974-H) | 4/05/29 | 4.00 |

**LUCAS, CLYDE**                                  NMP (.0-.50)

**LUNCEFORD, JIMMIE** and his orchestra
  Generally NMP, not including those below:

| | | | |
|---|---|---|---|
| Sweet Rhythm | (VIC V-38141) | 6/06/30 | 8.00 |
| Jazznocracy | (VIC 24522) | 1/26/34 | 7.00 |
| White Heat | (VIC 24586) | 1/26/34 | 7.00 |
| Swingin' Uptown | (VIC 24669) | 3/20/34 | 6.00 |
| For Dancers Only | (DEC 1340) | 6/15/37 | 3.50 |
| Margie | (DEC 1617) | 1/06/38 | 3.50 |
| Uptown Blues (theme) | (VOC 5362) | 12/14/39 | 3.50 |
| Lunceford Special | (VOC 5326) | 12/14/39 | 3.50 |
| Battle Axe | (DEC 3807) | 3/26/41 | 3.50 |
| Yard Dog Mazurka | (DEC 4032) | 8/26/41 | 3.50 |
| Blues in the Night (2 pts.) | (DEC 4125) | 12/22/41 | 3.50 |

**LUTHER, FRANK**                                NMP (.0-.25)

**LYMAN, ABE**                                   NMP (.0-.75)

# *INTERMISSION* 5

## *Black Friday: The 1942-44 Record Ban*

Historians of the swing era isolate the record ban of 1942-43-44 as a major contributing factor to the demise of the "big band" syndrome. Admittedly, there were other causes—the coming of WWII, curtailments of travel, loss of key personnel to the military, material shortages, the rise of the vocalist as primary interpreter of the wartime ethos, musical obsolescence, to cite a few—but the prohibition on cutting new records turned out to be the *coup de grâce*. By 1945 the complexion of pop music had changed to such an extent that the prospect of restoring big bands to their earlier preeminence was exceedingly remote. The December 30, 1948, edition of *Downbeat* headlined the question: "What Is the Matter with the Dance Band Business?" One answer among many is that big bands never recovered fully the momentum blunted by the ban.

How did this trauma come about? The ban took effect at midnight, Friday, July 31, 1942, but the story, not every aspect of which can be discussed here, opens long before the night the studios fell silent.

The American Federation of Musicians (AFM), chartered from the A.F. of L. in 1896, had but two presidents up to 1940. By 1921 it had brought all locals under its wing, sometimes exerting heavy psychological and physical pressure upon reluctant groups. Enter James C. Petrillo, who knew how to make believers of recalcitrants. Chicago born (1892) and bred, Petrillo was a man with a consuming purpose. His single-minded, assertive manner earned him the top post in the AFM's Chicago local (1922). Between 1930 and 1940 Petrillo pursued his special goal: forcing domestic record companies to compensate musicians in the form of royalties payable to the AFM. He advertised his larger intentions in 1937-38 by ordering a strike against Chicago-area record/transcription producers.

In June, 1940 Petrillo was elected third president of the powerful AFM and set out to "throttle the recording industry." He already had a strategy in mind. From his constituents, assembled in Dallas for the annual AFM convention (June, 1942), Petrillo extracted the authorization he needed. He then notified all the major record companies (and his AFM locals) that commencing August 1, 1942, no AFM member would participate in the making of transcriptions or musical discs. Petrillo slapped some very wealthy, influential corporations right across the mouth with a mail glove and dared them to defy him. His future, and theirs, were on the line.

At first Petrillo was not taken seriously. Few people believed he could make good on his threat. Certainly his edict would be withdrawn before the deadline, many thought. Elmer Davis of the OWI prevailed upon Petrillo to recant. Newspapers generally sympathized with the record companies and scolded Petrillo for his presumptuousness. But "Little Caesar" and his 140,000 faithful disciples refused to budge. When it dawned on the record industry that Petrillo meant to carry through, an orgy of eleventh-hour recording sessions began at studios in New York, Chicago, Hollywood, and Los Angeles. It was the twilight of the gods.

During the final week (July 24-31) the recording schedule was particularly heavy. Among those who rushed to get something on wax were: Count Basie, Woody Herman, Alvino Rey, Johnny Long, Claude Thornhill, Judy Garland, Bing Crosby, Glen Gray, Benny Goodman, Kay Kyser, Jan Savitt, Dick Jurgens, Shep Fields, Dinah Shore, Freddy Martin, Tommy Tucker, Tony Pastor, Harry James, Spike Jones, Duke Ellington, and Mitchell Ayres. Earlier in the month other luminaries cut their last new sides: Tommy Dorsey (July 1, 2); Bing Crosby (July 13, 19, 20); Charlie Barnet (July 17); Jimmy Dorsey (July 14); Guy Lombardo (July 3). In Chicago, Petrillo's hometown, Glenn Miller's orchestra took advantage of a stand at the Hotel Sherman (July 7-16) to cut its final thirteen sides. It took twelve hours over a three-day period (July 14-16) for Miller's band to record "Juke Box Saturday Night," "Rhapsody in Blue," and other gems. No one suspected that Miller was recording his last discs as a civilian bandleader.

The major companies tried a tactic and a strategy in an attempt to beat the ban. The tactic was to substitute vocal groups for instrumentalists. Backing for crooners such as Bing Crosby, Dick Haymes, Perry Como, and Frank Sinatra was supplied by the Ken Darby singers, Song Spinners, and similar "choruses" who tried desperately to duplicate the sounds of real orchestras. Petrillo objected to this unethical circumvention but he need not have worried all that much. The ersatz music never caught on. (If you wonder why, listen to Sinatra's "Close to You" on Columbia 36678 and/or Haymes' "It Can't Be Wrong" on Decca 18557.)

The strategy was called "stockpiling" and was based upon the assumption that the companies had a backlog of unreleased masters sufficient to outlast the ban. Capitol clearly did not, and sheer survival required that the young firm succumb to the AFM, which it did in October, 1943. Decca tried to hold out but without a classical catalog to rely upon it could not stretch out its wares long enough. Decca gave up in September, 1943. Both companies began to cut new releases promptly and their depleted coffers filled up rapidly.

Victor and Columbia, older but not much wiser as it developed, fought the ban for another year, certain that their resources would overcome Petrillo's intransigence over the long haul. Running short of unreleased material they took to re-issuing items previously recorded by Goodman, T. Dorsey, James, Martin, and other big names. (In some instances this retread policy produced some surprises. For example, Artie Shaw's "Now We Know," originally recorded as a "B" side on May 13, 1940, enjoyed an astonishing popularity when Victor brought it out of obscurity in 1943. So did "All or Nothing At All," another Victor/Columbia resurrection from 1939.) But these minor victories were simply not enough to sustain the Big Two. Shellac was available once more, Capitol and Decca were flourishing, and bankruptcy was rearing its fearsome head. Appropriately, on Armistice Day, 1944, Victor and Columbia signed agreements with the AFM and the record ban came to an end.

The *thermidor* period following the ban is as interesting as the battle of 1942-44. Petrillo was exultant. He was not beloved by any means but he had won some people's begrudging respect. After all, a 5'6", 190-pound David had kayoed the record industry Goliath. Without much external support he had defied public opinion, Congressional pressure, a steady stream of invective from the media, the Justice Department, and, yes, the weight of the White House—and won. In the wake of the despised Taft-Hartley Act (1947) Petrillo called for another ban which lasted throughout 1948. Its impact was more modest than its wartime predecessor. The record companies had learned a lesson from 1942 and stockpiled in depth, Petrillo had lost some of his luster by then, and public interest was at the ho-hum level. The differences were negotiated this time and the AFM settled down to savor its enriched employee fund. Petrillo retired from the presidency a decade later.

On balance the record industry did not suffer unduly from the 1942-44 ban. In fact record sales zoomed to 275 million and 400 million in 1946 and 1947 respectively (up from 127 million in 1941). There were some slumps to be endured still (1949-55) but the overall trend was upward and onward toward the conglomerate era. Today the record business hovers at the $4 billion per annum level.

The real victims of the ban were the big bands. Unable to record any freshly written tunes they experienced a hardening of their arteries. Complications set in, also. When the ban was lifted the bands discovered that they "were no longer champions of the recording field." By 1945 the public imagination had been captured by vocalists such as Sinatra, Como, Haymes, and Jo Stafford. Until the war most singers were props. After the war they became the stars and the role of the bands was gradually subordinated. As Leo Walker pointed out the "deterioration was relentless despite periodic optimistic declarations of impending prosperity and booms . . ." in the big band business. Of course some bands carried on into the 1970s (Ellington, Basie, Herman, Kenton) but the "big band era" *per se* was beyond recall. July 31, 1942 was Pearl Harbor day for that remarkable, irretrievable phenomenon.

---

Sources for further reading: Gelatt, *The Fabulous Phonograph*, op cit.; Robert D. Leiter, *The Musicians and Petrillo* (Octagon; New York; 1974), original 1953; George T. Simon, *The Big Bands* (Collier; New York; 1974), original 1967; Peter A. Soderbergh, "Moonlight and Shadows: The Big Bands, 1934-1974," *Midwest Quarterly* (Autumn, 1974), 85-96; Leo Walker, *The Wonderful Era of the Great Dance Bands* (Doubleday; New York; 1964), 139-161; *Fortune* (April 23, 1979), 58-68.

# M

**MADRIGUERA, ENRIC**        NMP (.0-.50)

**MAJESTIC DANCE ORCHESTRA**   NMP (.0-.20)

**MALNECK, MATTY**         NMP (.0-1.00)

**MANONE, WINGY** and his various groups
Generally NMP with these exceptions:

| | | | |
|---|---|---|---|
| Cat's Head | (COL 14282D) | 4/11/27 | $ 7.00 |
| Ringside Stomp | (COL 1044D) | 4/11/27 | 7.00 |
| Downright Disgusted (Krupa) | (VOC 15728) | 9/04/28 | 7.00 |
| Trying to Stop My Crying | (VOC 15797) | 12/17/28 | 6.50 |
| Up the Country Blues | (GEN 7320) | 9/19/30 | 8.00 |
| Tin Roof Blues | (CHA 16153) | 9/19/30 | 7.00 |
| Big Butter and Egg Man | (CHA 16192) | 9/19/30 | 7.00 |
| Strange Blues | | | |
|   (Bauduc, Matlock, E. Miller) | (BRN 6911) | 5/02/34 | 6.00 |
| Send Me | (BRN 6940) | 5/02/34 | 6.00 |
| Royal Garden Blues (N. Lamare) | (OKE 41570) | 10/03/34 | 8.00 |
| Just One Girl | (OKE 41569) | 10/03/34 | 8.00 |
| I've Got a Note | | | |
|   (Teagarden, J. Mercer) | (VOC 3071) | 10/17/35 | 7.50 |

**MARSHARD, JACK** and his orchestra
Unquestionably NMP but for these curiosities:

| | | | |
|---|---|---|---|
| My Love for You | | | |
|   (Vaughn Monroe vocal) | (BRN 8398) | 5/23/39 | 3.50 |
| In the Still of the Night (Monroe) | (BRN 8417) | 6/07/39 | 3.50 |

**MARTIN, FREDDY** and his orchestra
Generally NMP with these allowances:

| | | | |
|---|---|---|---|
| Goodbye to Love (B. Berigan) | (COL 2703D) | 8/24/32 | 5.00 |
| Nightfall (Berigan) | (COL 2708D) | 8/24/32 | 5.00 |
| Forbidden Love (Berigan) | (BRN 6408) | 10/14/32 | 4.50 |
| A Rainy Day (Berigan) | (BRN 6407) | 10/14/32 | 4.50 |
| Stars Fell on Alabama | | | |
|   (Buddy Clark) | (BRN 6976) | 9/14/34 | 5.00 |

**Freddy Martin**          Photograph courtesy Alf Hildman, West Des Moines

| Isn't It a Shame? (B. Clark) | (BRN 6982) | 9/14/34 | $ 3.50 |
| Bye-Lo-Bye Lullaby (theme) | (BLB 10104) | 11/06/38 | 3.00 |

## MARTIN, MARY
Generally NMP but for a few items such as:

| My Heart Belongs to Daddy | | | |
| (E. Duchin orch.) | (BRN 8282) | 11/30/38 | 3.50 |
| The Waiter and the Porter ... | | | |
| (Teagarden, Bing Crosby) | (DEC 3970) | 5/26/41 | 5.00 |
| Wait Till the Sun Shines, Nellie | | | |
| (Crosby) | (DEC 18278) | 3/13/42 | 4.00 |

**MARTIN, TONY**  NMP (.0-.50)

**MARVIN, JOHNNY**  NMP (.0-.50)

**MASTERS, FRANKIE**  NMP (.0-.25)

**MC COY, CLYDE**  NMP (.0-1.00)

## MC DONOUGH, DICK and his orchestra
Generally NMP except for these items of interest:

| Summer Holiday (Shaw, Berigan, | | | |
| Thornhill, B. Clark) | (ARC 6-09-07) | 6/23/36 | 4.00 |
| Dear Old Southland (as above) | (ARC 6-09-08) | 6/23/36 | 4.00 |
| It Ain't Right | | | |
| (Berigan, Clark, C. Cole) | (ARC 6-11-02) | 8/04/36 | 3.50 |
| Midnight Blue (Clark) | (ARC 6-11-04) | 8/05/36 | 3.00 |
| Afterglow (Clark) | (ARC 6-11-01) | 8/05/36 | 3.00 |
| The Big Apple (Berigan) | (ARC 7-11-02) | 9/02/37 | 3.50 |

**MC FARLAND TWINS**  NMP (.0-.20)

**MC INTYRE, HAL**  NMP (.0-1.25)

## MC KINNEY'S COTTON PICKERS

| Milenberg Joys | (VIC 21611) | 7/11/28 | 5.00 |
| Cherry | (VIC 21730) | 7/12/28 | 5.00 |
| It's Tight like That | (VIC V-38013) | 11/23/28 | 4.00 |
| Plain Dirt | (VIC V-38097) | 11/05/29 | 5.00 |

**Tony Martin**          Photograph courtesy Alf Hildman, West Des Moines

**Clyde McCoy**     Photograph courtesy Alf Hildman, West Des Moines

**The Bennett Sisters with Clyde McCoy**

Photograph courtesy Alf Hildman, West Des Moines

| Zonky | (VIC V-38118) | 2/03/30 | $ 5.00 |
| Okay, Baby | (VIC 23000) | 7/29/30 | 7.50 |
| Cotton Picker's Scat | (VIC 23012) | 7/31/30 | 7.00 |

**MC SHANN, JAY**　　　　　　　　NMP (.0-1.00)

**MERCER, JOHNNY**

Unfortunately NMP excepting these long shots:

| | | | |
| --- | --- | --- | --- |
| Dr. Heckle and Mr. Jibe | | | |
| (Dorsey Brothers) | (BRN 01834) | 10/17/33 | 5.00 |
| Fare-Thee-Well to Harlem | | | |
| (Whiteman, Teagarden) | (VIC 24571) | 2/16/34 | 4.00 |
| Christmas Night in Harlem | | | |
| (as above) | (VIC 24615) | 4/17/34 | 4.00 |
| I've Got a Note | | | |
| (Manone, Teagarden) | (VOC 3071) | 10/08/35 | 7.50 |
| Eeny Meeny Miney Mo | | | |
| (Ginger Rogers) | (DEC 638) | 11/27/35 | 6.00 |
| Small Fry (Bing Crosby) | (DEC 1960) | 7/01/38 | 5.00 |
| Sent for You Yesterday ... | | | |
| (Goodman) | (VIC 26170) | 2/01/39 | 3.50 |
| Mister Meadowlark | | | |
| (Bing Crosby) | (DEC 3182) | 4/15/40 | 5.00 |
| Old Music Master | | | |
| (Whiteman, Teagarden) | (CAP 137) | 6/12/42 | 3.00 |

| | | | |
|---|---|---|---|
| **MEROFF, BENNY** | NMP (.0-1.00) | | |
| **MERRY MACS, THE** | NMP (.0-.50) | | |
| **MESSNER JOHNNY** | NMP (.0-.50) | | |
| **MILLER, EDDIE** | NMP (.0-1.00) | | |

**MILLER, GLENN\*** and his orchestra

\*Miller presents this writer, at least, with a problem of interpretation. On the one hand he is such a legend, such a symbol that it is almost sacreligious to suggest that the bulk of his recorded output for BLB and VIC (1938-42) cannot be priced above the $3.50 level (due mainly to the availability of his material on LP). That is the case, as I see it, however painful it feels. I know that Miller buffs in the U.S.A. and England view all of his records as priceless and incomparable mementos of a beloved era and might be happy to pay dearly for an original Miller in M or VG condition. I tend to sympathize with people of that persuasion in my heart, but my head tells me that Miller discs (excepting those below) are not overly valuable in the cold, cruel marketplace. It is wonderful to own a stack of Miller records, but it is unwise to conclude that they are going to generate, as the saying goes, big bucks. The following discs are a matter of interest and may be assessed quite apart from the BLB-VIC standbys:

| | | | |
|---|---|---|---|
| A Blues Serenade | | | |
| (Spivak, Berigan, Bauduc) | (COL 3051D) | 4/25/35 | $10.00 |
| Solo Hop (as above) | (COL 3058D) | 4/25/35 | 10.00 |
| Moonlight Bay | (DEC 1239) | 3/22/37 | 4.00 |
| Wistful and Blue | (DEC 1284) | 3/22/37 | 4.00 |
| Peg O' My Heart | (DEC 1342) | 3/22/37 | 4.00 |
| I Got Rhythm | (BRN 7915) | 6/09/37 | 6.00 |
| Sleepy Time Gal | (BRN 7923) | 6/09/37 | 6.00 |
| My Fine Feathered Friend | (BRN 8034) | 11/29/37 | 6.00 |
| Doin' the Jive | (BRN 8062) | 11/29/37 | 6.00 |
| Every Day's a Holiday | (BRN 8041) | 12/13/37 | 6.00 |
| Don't Wake Up My Heart | (BRN 8152) | 5/23/38 | 6.00 |
| Dippermouth Blues | (BRN 8173) | 5/23/38 | 6.50 |

**Glenn Miller**          Photograph courtesy Alf Hildman, West Des Moines

**Russ Morgan**          Photograph courtesy Alf Hildman, West Des Moines

149

## MILLINDER, LUCKY

NMP (.0-1.00)

## MILLS BROTHERS, THE

| | | | |
|---|---|---|---|
| Tiger Rag | (BRN 6197) | 10/12/31 | $ 8.50 |
| Gems from George White's Scandals (12″) | (BRN 20102) | 10/25/31 | 10.00 |
| Dinah (Bing Crosby) | (BRN 6240) | 12/16/31 | 8.00 |
| Shine (Bing Crosby) | (BRN 6276) | 2/16/32 | 8.00 |
| O.K. America (12″) | (BRN 20112) | 4/14/32 | 6.00 |
| Diga Diga Doo (Ellington) | (BRN 6519) | 12/22/32 | 5.00 |
| Doin' the New Low-Down (Calloway) | (BRN 6517) | 12/29/32 | 4.00 |
| My Honey's Lovin' Arms (Bing Crosby) | (BRN 6525) | 1/26/33 | 8.00 |
| Darling Nellie Gray (Louis Armstrong) | (DEC 1245) | 4/07/37 | 3.00 |
| Flat Foot Floogie (Armstrong) | (DEC 1876) | 6/10/38 | 2.75 |
| Paper Doll | (DEC 18318) | 2/18/42 | 3.00 |

## MINEVITCH, BORAH

NMP (.0-.50)

## MIRANDA, CARMEN

NMP (.0-.50)

## MONROE, VAUGHN

NMP (.0-1.25)

## MORGAN, HELEN

| | | | |
|---|---|---|---|
| Bill | (VIC 21238) | 2/14/28 | 3.00 |
| Mean to Me | (VIC 21930) | 2/06/29 | 2.50 |
| More Than You Know | (VIC 22149) | 10/08/29 | 2.50 |
| Why Was I Born? | (VIC 22199) | 10/16/29 | 2.50 |
| Body and Soul | (VIC 22532) | 9/12/30 | 2.00 |
| Bill (Victor Young orch.) | (BRN 20115) | 8/09/32 | 2.50 |
| Winter Overnight (J. Grier orch.) | (BRN 7391) | 12/05/34 | 3.00 |

**MORGAN, RUSS** and his orchestra

Usually NMP but for these few early cuts:

| | | | |
|---|---|---|---|
| Washin' the Blues from My Soul | (ODE 36095) | 5/20/30 | $ 5.00 |
| I Remember You from Somewhere | (ODE 36097) | 5/20/30 | 5.00 |
| Little Sunshine | (ODE 36140) | 9/02/30 | 5.00 |

**MOTEN, BENNIE** and his orchestra

| | | | |
|---|---|---|---|
| Crawdad Blues | (OKE 8100) | 9/23 | 15.00 |
| South (theme) | (OKE 8194) | 11/29/24 | 15.00 |
| Tulsa Blues | (OKE 8184) | 11/29/24 | 10.00 |
| Baby Dear | (OKE 8213) | 11/29/24 | 10.00 |
| South Street Blues | (OKE 8255) | 5/14/25 | 10.00 |
| 18th Street Strut | (OKE 8242) | 5/14/25 | 10.00 |
| Thick Lip Stomp | (VIC 20406) | 12/13/26 | 6.00 |
| Kansas City Shuffle | (VIC 20485) | 12/13/26 | 6.00 |
| Midnight Mama | (VIC 20422) | 12/14/26 | 5.00 |
| Sugar | (VIC 20855) | 6/11/27 | 5.00 |
| Twelfth Street Rag | (VIC 20946) | 6/11/27 | 5.00 |
| Moten Stomp | (VIC 20955) | 6/12/27 | 10.00 |
| Kansas City Breakdown | (VIC 21693) | 9/07/28 | 7.00 |
| Moten's Blues | (VIC V-38072) | 7/17/29 | 6.00 |
| Band Box Shuffle (C. Basie) | (VIC 23007) | 10/23/29 | 8.00 |
| Won't You Be My Baby? (J. Rushing, O. Page) | (VIC 23028) | 10/27/30 | 8.00 |
| The Count | (VIC 23391) | 10/28/30 | 8.00 |
| New Moten Stomp | (VIC 23030) | 10/30/30 | 8.00 |
| Somebody Stole My Gal | (VIC 23028) | 10/31/30 | 5.00 |
| Moten Swing | (VIC 23384) | 12/13/32 | 5.00 |

**MUNN, FRANK**          NMP (.0-.25)

**MURRAY, KEL**          NMP (.0-.20)

# *INTERMISSION* 6

## *250 Theme Songs from the 78 rpm Era*

Nothing brings the Big Dance Bands to the forefront of the imagination so quickly as a famous theme song. A few bars of *Let's Dance, Day Dreams Come True at Night,* or *Smoke Rings* and the years fall away. Suddenly, it is November, 1939 — or some other precious time we have preserved in our minds.

There we are again on the crowded floor of a college gymnasium, or pressed up against the bandstand at the Meadowbrook — oblivious to Depression, chronology, and war — drinking in every note blown our way by the traveling ambassadors of sweet and swing. Romance, tragedy, and ecstasy interweave for a moment as we go spinning back — and then the cherished images depart (as all memories do) for some uncharted region within us. It does not take much to conjure it all up again, however. Twenty seconds of Tommy Dorsey's *I'm Getting Sentimental over You* will do the trick. It is absolutely Pavlovian.

Some theme songs — *Moonlight Serenade* being a prime example — represent much more than the aura of a particular orchestra. The young people of the thirties and forties related so strongly to certain musical signatures that even today, should a key theme be played, they are overtaken by a tidal wave of sentiment. Identification of that magnitude says something about the impact of the Big Band ethos on the public consciousness. It was very powerful. And why not? An entire generation cut its teeth on the three R's: Records, Radio, and Recreation. The Big Bands came to us that way. We played their records on the family phonograph, devoured their coast-to-coast broadcasts, and drove many miles in fragile jalopies to see them in person. The crowning point in our mounting anticipation came when the first strains of that well-known theme song burst over our sensibilities. It was an invitation to an hour or two of stroboscopic thrills. It was unforgettable.

In this section I present 250 artists whose theme songs received a good deal of exposure between 1935 and 1945. In some instances I make comments which I hope will add substance to the list. You may not recognize each and every theme, but — rest assured — there is a fan for every one. Somebody out there really cares for his or her favorite, just as you do. If you have any of these discs in your collection, keep them. They may not be emeralds exactly, but they say more about the heyday of 78's than other 78 records I know. The song may be ended. These melodies linger on. As Dick Jurgens' announcer used to say: ''Here's that band again!''

| Artist | Theme Song |
|---|---|
| AARONSON, Irving | Commanderism |
| ALEXANDER, Van | Alexander's Ragtime Band |
| ALLEN, Henry ''Red'' | Way Down Yonder in New Orleans/ The Crawl |
| AMBROSE, Bert | Hors d'Oeuvres/Tarantula |
| A & P GYPSIES | Two Guitars |
| ARCARAZ, Luis | Sombra Verde |
| ARMSTRONG, Louis | When It's Sleepy Time Down South |

First recorded on OKE 41504 (4/20/31) this ingratiating theme did not become readily available to the record-buying public until Armstrong cut it for DEC (4140) on 11/16/41. *Sleepy Time* abridged may also be heard on VIC 36084 (12/21/32) as one of Armstrong's Medley of Hits (12").

| ARNAZ, Desi | Cuban Pete |
|---|---|
| ARNHEIM, Gus | Sweet and Lovely/Say It with Music |
| ASTOR, Bob | Blue Lights |
| AULD, Georgie | I've Got a Right to Know |
| AYRES, Mitchell | You Go to My Head |
| | |
| BALLEW, Smith | Tonight There is Music in the Air/Home |
| BARGY, Roy | Sunshine Capers/Pianoflage |
| BARNET, Charlie | Cherokee/Redskin Rhumba |

Prior to recording Ray Noble's *Cherokee* (BLB 10373) on 7/17/39 Barnet's orchestra employed *I Lost Another Sweetheart* as its theme song. *Cherokee*, of course, was more representative of the band's musical inclinations between 1939 and 1942. After 1940, Barnet sometimes used *Redskin Rhumba* as an alternate signature. On 8/12/46 he cut *Cherokee* and *New Redskin Rhumba* on CAR 25001.

| Artist | Theme Song |
|--------|------------|
| BARRON, Blue | Sometimes I'm Happy |
| BASIE, Count | One O'clock Jump/Rock-a-Bye Basie |

*Jump* may be found on DEC 1363 (7/7/37) or on OKE 6634 (1/21/42). It is interesting to note that Benny Goodman's more popular version (VIC 25792) was not recorded until 2/16/38 and, it appears, was arranged by Basie.

| | |
|--------|------------|
| BECHET, Sidney | Summertime/Blues of Bechet |
| BEIDERBECKE, Bix | In a Mist/At the Jazz Band Ball |
| BENEKE, Tex | Moonlight Serenade |
| BERIGAN, Bunny | I Can't Get Started with You |

First put on a 12″ disc, VIC 36208 (8/7/37), this Berigan classic was subsequently (and, unsatisfactorily) dubbed onto a 10″ record (VIC 25728), which a collector should avoid. Among Berigan's sidemen during this session were Steve Lipkins, George Wettling, Georgie Auld, and Joe Lippman.

| | |
|--------|------------|
| BERNIE, Ben | Au Revoir/It's a Lonesome Old Town |

The "Old Maestro's" closing theme, *Au Revoir-Pleasant Dreams,* was equally as prominent as *Lonesome Old Town,* perhaps, due to Bernie's spoken vocal in which his famous "Yowsah" was featured. In 1951 DEC (25282) re-released both themes on one disc.

| | |
|--------|------------|
| BESTOR, Don | Teach Me to Smile |
| BIGARD, Barney | Barney Goin' Easy |
| BLOCH, Ray | Music in My Fingers/Espanharlem |
| BOSTIC, Earl | The Bostic Jump/Away |
| BRADLEY, Will | Think of Me |

The original record of this beautiful ballad (COL 36101; 1/30/41) includes a bonus. On the reverse side is a jazz masterpiece, *Tea for Two,* by the Ray McKinley Quartet (McKinley, Doc Goldberg, Freddie Slack, and "Peanuts" Hucko), recorded on 1/21/41.

| | |
|--------|------------|
| BRADSHAW, Tiny | Fascination/Bradshaw Bounce |
| BRANDWYNNE, Nat | If Stars Could Talk/Whispers in the Night |
| BREESE, Lou | Breezin' Along with the Breeze |
| BRIGODE, Ace | Carry Me Back to Old Virginny |
| BRING, Lou | Love Rides on the Moon |
| BROOKS, Randy | Harlem Nocturne/Holiday Forever |

| Artist | Theme Song |
|---|---|

**BROWN, Les**          Leap Frog/Sentimental Journey

> Leap Frog (COL 36857; 1945) was one of Brown's themes. The other,
> Sentimental Journey, with vocal by Doris Day, became one of the
> foremost symbols of the World War II era.

**BRYANT, Willie**         It's Over Because We're Through
**BUSSE, Henry**          Hot Lips/When Day Is Done
**BUTTERFIELD, Billy**       What's New?/Moonlight in Vermont

> When Butterfield formed his orchestra in 1946, he adopted *What's New?*
> as his theme for good reason. While he was with the Bob Crosby band
> Butterfield played the trumpet solo part of Bob Haggart's lyrical com-
> position *I'm Free* (DEC 2205; 10/19/38). Words were added to this
> instrumental and it became *What's New? (Pardon, if I'm boring
> you . . .)*, a minor jazz classic.

**BUTTERFIELD, Erskine**    Rhapsody in Love
**BYRNE, Bobby**          Danny Boy

**CALLOWAY, Cab**         Minnie the Moocher
**CARLE, Frankie**         Sunrise Serenade

> By the time Frankie Carle finally formed his own band in February,
> 1944, *Sunrise Serenade* (his own composition) had already done more
> for others than for him. Glenn Miller's rendition (BLB 10214; 4/10/39),
> backed by *Moonlight Serenade*, sold a million copies and helped Miller
> capture much public attention. Glen Gray's version on DEC 2321
> (2/17/39) was overwhelmed by Miller's record — even though it fea-
> tured Carle on the piano for that particular session.

**CARMICHAEL, Hoagy**     Stardust
**CARROLL, Jimmy**        I Hear America Singing
**CARTER, Benny**         Melancholy Lullaby/Malibu
**CASA LOMA**
**ORCHESTRA**           (See GRAY, Glen)
**CAVALLARO, Carmen**     My Sentimental Heart/Chopin's Polonaise
**CHESTER, Bob**         Sunburst
**CLINTON, Larry**        Dipsy Doodle/Study in Brown

> Strangely enough, Larry "The Old Dipsy Doodler" Clinton, never
> recorded his own theme song (and creation) during the Big Band era. The
> reason was this: Tommy Dorsey cut the *Dipsy Doodle* on VIC 25693
> (10/14/37). In fact, Clinton arranged it for Dorsey before he organized

155

his own orchestra in 1938. Since they were both on the VIC label, it was deemed unwise to release competitive recordings of the same tune — so Clinton could play his composition during public appearances and broadcasts only.

| | |
|---|---|
| COBURN, Jolly | There's Music in the Stars |
| CONFREY, Zez | Kitten on the Keys |
| COON-SANDERS ORCH. | Night Hawk Blues |
| COURTNEY, Del | Good Evening/Three Shades of Blue |
| CRAIG, Francis | Near You/Red Rose |
| CROSBY, Bob | Summertime |
| CUGAT, Xavier | My Shawl |

There is an earlier version (1933) of this bolero on VIC, but Cugat's 1945 record (COL 36842) with vocal by an emerging Frank Sinatra is by far most desirable from a collector's point of view.

| | |
|---|---|
| CUMMINS, Bernie | Dark Eyes |
| DAILEY, Frank | Gypsy Violin |
| DE LANGE, Eddie | Don't Forget |
| DENNY, Jack | Under the Stars |
| DONAHUE, Al | Low Down Rhythm in a Top Hat |
| DONAHUE, Sam | Minor Deluxe/Lonesome |
| DORSEY BROTHERS ORCH. | Sandman |
| DORSEY, Jimmy | Contrasts |

Jimmy Dorsey's splendid theme was not recorded until 4/30/40 (DEC 3198). Its other side, *Perfidia*, was cut on 5/10/40. Together they constitute the Dorsey band at its instrumental best.

| | |
|---|---|
| DORSEY, Tommy | I'm Getting Sentimental over You |

George Simon was of the opinion that: "In retrospect — and in big band history — Tommy Dorsey's must be recognized as the greatest all-around dance band of them all." Simon might get an argument on that point, but few would disagree that T.D.'s touching theme song (VIC 25236; 10/17/35) ranks among the top three in pop music history.

| | |
|---|---|
| DUCHIN, Eddy | My Twilight Dream |

| Artist | Theme Song |
|---|---|

**DUNHAM, Sonny**     Memories of You

Dunham's association with this song began with his trumpet solo on DEC 1672 (12/1/37), while with Glen Gray's Casa Loma orchestra. He formed his own band in February, 1940 and cut two more versions of *Memories:* VAR 8234 (March, 1940) and BLB 11239 (7/23/41), either of which is worth having if the 1937 version is unavailable.

**ELDRIDGE, Ray**     Little Jazz/After You've Gone
**ELLINGTON, Duke**     East St. Louis Toodle-Oo/
Take the "A" Train

For 14 years (1927-41) Ellington used *East St. Louis Toodle-Oo* as his theme, recording it on BRN, COL, PAR, and DIVA. After 1941, *"A" Train* (VIC 27380; 2/15/41) predominated.

**ELMAN, Ziggy**     Zaggin' with Zig/And the Angels Sing
**ENNIS, Skinnay**     Got a Date with an Angel/
Same Time, Same Place
**FIELDS, Shep**     Rippling Rhythm/Ritual Fire Dance
**FIO RITO, Ted**     Rio Rita
**FISHER, Freddy**     Colonel Corn
**FOMEEN, Basil**     Manhattan Gypsy
**FOSTER, Chuck**     Oh, You Beautiful Doll
**FUNK, Larry**     Rose of Washington Square

**GARBER, Jan**     My Dear
**GOLDKETTE, Jean**     The Old Refrain/I Know That You Know
**GOODMAN, Al**     Till We Meet Again
**GOODMAN, Benny**     Goodbye/Let's Dance

Goodman's first theme was a baleful interpretation of Gordon Jenkins' *Goodbye* (VIC 25215; 9/27/35). It was replaced by the cheerful, symbolic *Let's Dance* shortly after he signed with the new Columbia label. The original of the latter is COL 35301 (10/24/39) and includes performers such as Charlie Christian, Ziggy Elman, Toots Mondello, Nick Fatool, Fletcher Henderson, and Vernon Brown.

**GORDON, Gray**     One Minute to One
**GRAY, Glen**     Was I to Blame?/Smoke Rings

*Smoke Rings* was recorded by Casa Loma the first time on 3/18/32 (BRN 6289). The famous rendition was cut on 7/23/37 (DEC 1473) and

| Artist | Theme Song |
| --- | --- |

featured Billy Rausch on trombone. Casa Loma had an earlier theme: *Was I to Blame for Falling in Love with You?* (BRN 6263; 2/18/32), sung by the great Kenny Sargent (who joined the band in 1931 and departed it in 1943).

GREEN, Larry — My Promise to You
GRIER, Jimmie — Music in the Moonlight/
Let's Dance and Dream

HALL, George — Love Letters in the Sand
HALLETT, Mal — The Boston Tea Party/Bay State Shuffle
HALSTEAD, Henry — Cuddle Up a Little Closer
HAMP, Johnny — My Old Kentucky Home
HAMPTON, Lionel — Flying Home

Any one of three recordings of *Flying Home* (VIC 26595; 2/26/40; DEC 18394; 5/26/42; DEC 23639; 3/2/44) are satisfactory, but the 1942 disc was the most popular.

HARRIS, Phil — Rose Room/Sunday/Persian Market
HAWKINS, Coleman — Body and Soul/Honeysuckle Rose
HAWKINS, Erskine — Tippin' In/Tuxedo Junction/Swing Out
HAYMES, Joe — Midnight
HEIDT, Horace — I'll Love You in My Dreams
HENDERSON, Fletcher — Christopher Columbus/Alabamy Bound

Henderson recorded *Columbus* for VOC (3211) on 3/27/36. One week earlier Benny Goodman cut a Henderson-arranged version (VIC 25279) which became much more popular, and some aspects of which he incorporated into Jimmy Mundy's arrangement of the 12" classic, *Sing, Sing, Sing,* (VIC 36205; 7/6/37).

HENDERSON, Horace — Chris and His Gang
HERBECK, Ray — Romance
HERMAN, Woody — Blue Flame/Woodchopper's Ball

*Flame* (DEC 2/13/41) was superseded by *Woodchopper's Ball,* which had been recorded several years before (DEC 2440; 4/12/39).

HEYWOOD, Eddie — Begin the Beguine/Orchids to You
HICKMAN, Art — Rose Room
HILL, Tiny — Angry
HIMBER, Richard — It Isn't Fair

| Artist | Theme Song |
|---|---|
| HINES, Earl | Deep Forest/Rosetta |
| HITE, Les | It Must Have Been a Dream |
| HODGES, Johnny | Day Dream |
| HOFF, Carl | I Could Use a Dream |
| HOPKINS, Claude | I Would Do Almost Anything for You |
| HORLICK, Harry | Black Eyes |
| HOWARD, Eddy | Careless |
| HUDSON, Dean | Moon over Miami |
| HUDSON-DELANGE ORCH. | Eight Bars in Search of a Melody |
| HUDSON, Will | Hobo on Park Avenue |
| HUTTON, Ina Ray | Gotta Have Your Love |
| HYLTON, Jack | She Shall Have Music/ Come Listen to the Band |
| | |
| IONA, Andy | South Sea Island |
| | |
| JAMES, Harry | Ciribiribin |
| JARRETT, Art | Everything's Been Done Before |
| JENNEY, Jack | City Night |
| JEROME, Henry | Nice People/Night Is Gone |
| JOHNSON, Johnny | If I Could Be with You One Hour Tonight |
| JONES, Isham | You're Just a Dream Come True |
| JONES, Spike | Cocktails for Two/Sheik of Araby |
| JORDAN, Louis | Pinetop's Boogie Woogie |
| JOY, Jimmy | My Darling/Shine On, Harvest Moon |
| JURGENS, Dick | Day Dreams Come True at Night |
| | |
| KAHN, Roger Wolfe | Where the Wild, Wild Flowers Grow |
| KARDOS, Gene | Business in F |
| KASSEL, Art | Hell's Bells/Doodle-Doo-Doo |
| KAVELIN, Al | Love Is Gone |
| KAY, Herbie | Violets and Friends |
| KAYE, Sammy | Kaye's Melody/Until Tomorrow |
| KEMP, Hal | Got a Date with an Angel/ When Summer Is Gone |

| Artist | Theme Song |
|---|---|
| KENTON, Stan | Artistry in Rhythm |
| KEPPARD, Freddie | Salty Dog |
| KING, Henry | A Blues Serenade |
| KING, Wayne | The Waltz You Saved for Me |
| KINNEY, Ray | Aloha Oe/Hawaii Across the Sea |
| KIRBY, John | Pastel Blue |
| KIRK, Andy | Clouds/Until the Real Thing Comes Along |
| KNAPP, Orville | Indigo/Accent on Youth |
| KRUPA, Gene | Apurksody/Starburst |

*Apurksody* (Krupa spelled backwards + sody) was cut on 12/12/38 (BRN 8296). In the late war years Krupa switched to *Star Burst*.

| | |
|---|---|
| KYSER, Kay | Thinking of You |

| | |
|---|---|
| LANIN, Sam | A Smile Will Go a Long, Long Way |
| LAWRENCE, Elliot | Heart to Heart |
| LEONARD, Harlan | A Mellow Bit of Rhythm/Southern Fried |
| LEWIS, Ted | When My Baby Smiles at Me |
| LIGHT, Enoch | You Are My Lucky Star |
| LOMBARDO, Guy | Auld Lang Syne |
| LONG, Johnny | White Star of Sigma Nu |
| LOPEZ, Vincent | Nola |

Lopez' trademark was composed by Felix Arndt (b. 1882), a talented pianist who made six rare ragtime records for VIC commencing in 1912. Arndt died in the great influenza epidemic of 1918, the very year Lopez was forming his first big band.

| | |
|---|---|
| LOWN, Bert | Bye Bye Blues |
| LUCAS, Clyde | Dance Mood |
| LUNCEFORD, Jimmie | Uptown Blues/Jazznocracy |

This driving, exciting instrumental (VIC 24522; 1/26/34), arranged by Will Hudson, served as Lunceford's theme until it was displaced by *Uptown Blues* (VOC 5362; 12/14/39).

| | |
|---|---|
| LYMAN, Abe | La Golondrina/California, Here I Come |

| | |
|---|---|
| MADRIGUERA, Enric | Adios |
| MALNECK, Matty | Park Avenue Fantasy/Stairway to the Stars |

160

| Artist | Theme Song |
|---|---|
| MARTIN, Freddy | Bye-Lo Bye Lullaby/<br>Piano Concerto in B Flat |

*Bye Lo*, a rather turgid, uninspiring piece, gave way to the million-selling *Piano Concerto in B Flat (Tonight We Love)* in 1941 (BLB 11211), which catapulted Martin into the limelight he had sought since organizing his band in 1933.

| Artist | Theme Song |
|---|---|
| MASTERS, Frankie | Scatterbrain/Moonlight and You |
| MC COY, Clyde | Sugar Blues |
| MC FARLAND TWINS | Darkness |
| MC INTIRE, Lani | You're the One Rose |
| MC INTYRE, Hal | Moon Mist/Ecstasy |
| MC KINLEY, Ray | Howdy, Friends |
| MC KINNEY'S COTTON PICKERS | If I Could Be with You One Hour Tonight |
| MC SHANN, Jay | Jiggin' with Jay/Confessin' the Blues |
| MEROFF, Benny | Diane |
| MESSNER, Johnny | Can't We Be Friends? |
| MILLINDER, Lucky | The Lucky Swing/Ride, Red, Ride |
| MILLER, Glenn | Moonlight Serenade/Slumber Song |

Miller wrote this melody while he was with Ray Noble in the mid-1930s, but it was not until lyricist Mitchell Parrish tried his hand at the words that *Moonlight Serenade* took shape early in 1939. Miller recorded it on 4/4/39 (BLB 10214) and the rest is history. His alternate theme during the days of the ASCAP-BMI wars was *Slumber Song* (BLB 11386; 11/24/41), but it did not strike the public's fancy to any significant degree.

| Artist | Theme Song |
|---|---|
| MONROE, Vaughn | Racing with the Moon |
| MOONEY, Art | Sunset to Sunrise |
| MORGAN, Russ | Does Your Heart Beat for Me? |
| MOTEN, Benny | South |
| | |
| NELSON, Ozzie | Loyal Sons of Rutgers |
| NEWMAN, Ruby | Rainbow in the Night |
| NICHOLS, Red | Wail of the Winds/Ida |
| NOBLE, Leighton | I'll See You in My Dreams |
| NOBLE, Ray | The Very Thought of You |

| Artist | Theme Song |
|---|---|
| NORVO, Red | I Surrender, Dear |
| | |
| OHMAN, Phil | Canadian Capers |
| OLIVER, King | Dippermouth Blues |
| OLSEN, George | Beyond the Blue Horizon |
| OSBORNE, Will | The Gentleman Awaits |
| OWENS, Harry | Sweet Leilani/Hawaii Calls |
| | |
| PALMER, Jimmy | It's a Lonesome Old Town |
| PASTOR, Tony | Blossoms |
| PEARL, Ray | A Kiss from Me to You |
| PENDARVIS, Paul | My Sweetheart |
| PHILLIPS, Teddy | Thankful |
| POLLACK, Ben | Song of the Islands |
| POWELL, Teddy | Blue Sentimental Mood |
| PRIMA, Louis | Way Down Yonder in New Orleans |
| | |
| RAEBURN, Boyd | Raeburn's Theme/Man with a Horn |
| RAVAZZA, Carl | Vieni Su |
| REDMAN, Don | Chant of the Weed/Cherry |
| REICHMAN, Joe | Pagliacci/Variations in G |
| REISMAN, Leo | What Is This Thing Called Love? |
| RENARD, Jacques | Coronet |
| REY, Alvino | Blue Rey/Nighty-Night |
| REYNOLDS, Tommy | Pipe Dreams |
| RICH, Freddie | So Beats My Heart for You |
| RILEY-FARLEY ORCH. | Music Goes 'Round and 'Round |
| ROGERS, Buddy | My Buddy |
| ROSE, David | Our Waltz/One Love |
| | |
| SAVITT, Jan | Quaker City Jazz |
| SCOTT, Raymond | Pretty Little Petticoat/Toy Trumpet |
| SENTER, Boyd | Bad Habits |
| SHAW, Artie | Nightmare |
| SHERWOOD, Bobby | Elk's Parade/Sherwood's Forest |
| SHILKRET, Nat | Dusky Stevedore |

| Artist | Theme Song |
|---|---|
| SISSLE, Noble | Hello, Sweetheart, Hello |
| SLACK, Freddie | Strange Cargo |
| SMITH, Joseph C. | Tulip Time |
| SOSNIK, Harry | Lazy Rhapsody |
| SPANIER, Muggsy | Relaxin' at the Touro |
| SPECHT, Paul | Evening Star/Sweetheart Time |
| SPITALNY, Phil | My Isle of Golden Dreams |
| SPIVAK, Charlie | Stardreams |
| STABILE, Dick | Blue Nocturne |
| STEELE, Blue | Coronado Memories |
| STRAETER, Ted | The Most Beautiful Girl in the World |
| STRONG, Benny | That Old Gang of Mine/That Certain Party |
| SWEATMAN, Wilbur | Battleship Kate |
| | |
| TATE, Erskine | Static Street |
| TEAGARDEN, Jack | I've Got a Right to Sing the Blues |

Teagarden's soulful theme, enhanced by his splendid vocal, was cut first on BRN 8397 (4/28/39) and then combined with *United We Swing* on OKE 6272 (10/6/39).

| Artist | Theme Song |
|---|---|
| THORNHILL, Claude | Snowfall |
| TRACE, Al | You Call Everybody Darlin'/Mairzy Doats |
| TREMAINE, Paul | Lonely Acres |
| TRUMBAUER, Frankie | Singin' the Blues |
| TUCKER, Orrin | Drifting and Dreaming |
| TUCKER, Tommy | I Love You |
| | |
| VALLEE, Rudy | My Time Is Your Time |
| VAN, Garwood | Poinciana/Time to Dream |
| VENUTI, Joe | Last Night |
| | |
| WALD, Jerry | Call of the Wild |
| WALLER, Fats | Ain't Misbehavin' |
| WARING, Fred | Sleep |
| WARNOW, Mark | Let's Play Make Believe |
| WEBB, Chick | I May Be Wrong |
| WEEKS, Anson | I'm Sorry, Dear |

**Tommy Dorsey**

Photograph courtesy RCA Victor

| Artist | Theme Song |
|---|---|
| WEEMS, Ted | Out of the Night |
| WELK, Lawrence | Bubbles in the Wine |
| WHITEMAN, Paul | Rhapsody in Blue |
| WIEDOFT, Rudy | Saxophobia |
| WILLIAMS, Griff | Dream Music |
| WILLSON, Meredith | You and I/Thoughts While Strolling |
| WILSON, Teddy | In a Mood |
| | |
| YANKOVIC, Frankie | Just Because |
| YOUNG, Victor | Sweet Sue |
| | |
| ZURKE, Bob | Southern Exposure/Hobson Street Blues |

# N

**NELSON, OZZIE**  NMP (.0-1.00)

**NEWMAN, RUBY**  NMP (.0-.75)

**NEW ORLEANS RHYTHM KINGS**

| | | | |
|---|---|---|---|
| Eccentric | (GEN 5009) | 8/29/22 | $ 50.00 |
| Farewell Blues | (GEN 4966) | 8/29/22 | 50.00 |
| Discontented Blues | (GEN 4967) | 8/29/22 | 50.00 |
| Tiger Rag (Brunies) | (GEN 4968) | 8/30/22 | 50.00 |
| Sweet Lovin' Man | | | |
| (Pollack, Brunies) | (GEN 5104) | 3/12/23 | 50.00 |
| That's a Plenty | (GEN 5105) | 3/12/23 | 50.00 |
| Da Da Strain | (GEN 5106) | 3/13/23 | 50.00 |
| Wolverine Blues | (GEN 5102) | 3/13/23 | 50.00 |
| Sobbin' Blues (J.R. Morton) | (GEN 5219) | 7/17/23 | 75.00 |
| Clarinet Marmalade (Morton) | (GEN 5220) | 7/17/23 | 75.00 |
| London Blues (Morton) | (GEN 5221) | 7/18/23 | 75.00 |
| Milenberg Joys (Morton) | (GEN 5217) | 7/18/23 | 75.00 |
| Baby | (OKE 40422) | 1/23/25 | 50.00 |
| Golden Leaf Strut | (OKE 40327) | 1/23/25 | 50.00 |
| Baby Brown | | | |
| (Spanier, Krupa, E. Miller) | (DEC 401) | 2/20/35 | 5.00 |
| Dust Off That Old Piano (as | | | |
| above) | (DEC 388) | 2/20/35 | 5.00 |

**NICHOLS, RED** and his various groups

| | | | |
|---|---|---|---|
| Alabama Stomp (Mole, J. Dorsey) | (EDI 51854) | 10/13/26 | 15.00 |
| Hurricane (as above) | (EDI 51878) | 11/10/26 | 15.00 |
| Washboard Blues | | | |
| (J. Dorsey, E. Lang) | (VOC 15498) | 12/08/26 | 10.00 |
| Bugle Call Rag | | | |
| (Mole, Venuti, J. Dorsey) | (BRN 3490) | 3/03/27 | 10.00 |
| Riverboat Shuffle | | | |
| (Mole, P.W. Russell) | (BRN 3627) | 8/15/27 | 10.00 |
| Sugar (Trumbauer, Russell) | (VIC 21056) | 10/26/27 | 8.00 |
| Poor Butterfly | (BRN 20062) | 3/02/28 | 10.00 |
| Limehouse Blues | (BRN 20070) | 5/31/28 | 10.00 |
| Five Pennies | (VIC 21560) | 6/21/28 | 8.00 |

| | | | |
|---|---|---|---|
| I Never Knew (Mole, Goodman) | (BRN 4243) | 2/01/29 | $ 8.00 |
| Indiana (G. Miller, Krupa, Goodman) | (BRN 4373) | 4/18/29 | 10.00 |
| It Had to Be You (Miller, J. Dorsey, Teagarden) | (BRN 20092) | 6/07/29 | 8.00 |
| Smiles (Goodman, Miller, J. Dorsey, Tough) | (BRN 4790) | 9/09/29 | 8.00 |
| Soon (Dorseys, Miller, Krupa) | (BRN 4695) | 1/17/30 | 10.00 |
| China Boy (Miller, Goodman, Teagarden) | (BRN 4877) | 7/02/30 | 8.00 |
| On Revival Day (Miller, Goodman, Krupa) | (BRN 6026) | 9/26/30 | 8.00 |
| That's Where the South Begins (as above) | (VIC 23026) | 11/18/30 | 8.00 |
| Rockin' Chair (Miller, Manone, J. Dorsey) | (BRN 6012) | 12/01/30 | 8.00 |
| California Medley (2 pts.) (Dorseys, Venuti, Boswells) | (BRN 20107) | 3/10/32 | 10.00 |

**NOBLE, LEIGHTON**                    NMP (.0-.50)

**NOBLE, RAY** and his orchestra
Generally NMP with these interesting exceptions:

| | | | |
|---|---|---|---|
| Soon (Spivak, Miller, Thornhill, W. Bradley) | (VIC 24879) | 2/09/35 | 5.00 |
| Clouds (as above) | (VIC 24865) | 2/09/35 | 5.00 |
| Chinatown, My Chinatown (as above) | (VIC 25070) | 6/10/35 | 5.00 |
| St. Louis Blues (as above) | (VIC 25082) | 6/10/35 | 5.00 |
| Bugle Call Rag (as above) | (VIC 25223) | 10/09/35 | 5.00 |

**NORVO, RED*** and his various groups

| | | | |
|---|---|---|---|
| Knockin' on Wood (J. Dorsey) | (BRN 6562) | 4/08/33 | 8.00 |
| In a Mist (Goodman) | (BRN 6098) | 11/21/33 | 8.00 |
| I Surrender Dear (Shaw, Barnet, Jenney) | (COL 2977D) | 9/26/34 | 9.00 |
| Honeysuckle Rose (Berigan, Krupa, Berry) | (COL 3059D) | 1/25/35 | 7.00 |

*Norvo's records were also released on CHA as "Kal Kenney" and "Len Herman" and their orchestras. Norvo discs for BRN, VOC, and COL (1936-42), featuring vocalist-wife Mildred Bailey, fall into the $2.50-4.00 range as a rule.

# O

**OLIVER, KING** and his various groups

| | | | |
|---|---|---|---|
| Canal Street Blues | (GEN 5133) | 4/06/23 | 150.00 |
| Mandy Lee Blues | (GEN 5134) | 4/06/23 | 150.00 |
| Chimes Blues | (GEN 5135) | 4/06/23 | 150.00 |
| Weather Bird Rag | (GEN 5132) | 4/06/23 | 150.00 |
| Snake Rag | (GEN 5184) | 4/06/23 | 100.00 |
| High Society Rag | (OKE 4933) | 6/22/23 | 150.00 |
| Sobbin' Blues | (OKE 4906) | 6/22/23 | 150.00 |
| Dipper Mouth Blues (theme) | (OKE 4918) | 6/23/23 | 150.00 |
| Jazzin' Babies' Blues | (OKE 4975) | 6/23/23 | 50.00 |
| Aligator Hop | (GEN 5274) | 10/05/23 | 150.00 |
| Zulus Ball | (GEN 5275) | 10/05/23 | 150.00 |
| If You Want My Heart | (GEN 5276) | 10/05/23 | 125.00 |
| Camp Meeting Blues | (COL 14003D) | 10/16/23 | 40.00 |
| New Orleans Stomp | (COL 13003D) | 10/16/23 | 40.00 |
| Buddy's Habit | (OKE 40000) | 10/25/23 | 75.00 |
| Room Rent Blues | (OKE 8148) | 10/25/23 | 70.00 |
| Riverside Blues | (OKE 40034) | 10/26/23 | 50.00 |
| Mabel's Dream | (OKE 8235) | 10/26/23 | 100.00 |
| Mabel's Dream | (PAR 20292) | 12/24/23 | 75.00 |
| The Southern Stomps | (PAR 12088) | 12/24/23 | 75.00 |
| King Porter | (AUT 617) | 12/24 | 100.00 |
| Too Bad | (VOC 1007) | 3/11/26 | 40.00 |
| Sugar Foot Stomp | (VOC 1033) | 5/29/26 | 40.00 |
| Dead Man Blues | (VOC 1059) | 9/17/26 | 35.00 |
| Doctor Jazz | (VOC 1113) | 4/22/27 | 35.00 |

| | | | |
|---|---|---|---|
| Showboat Shuffle | (VOC 1114) | 4/22/27 | $ 35.00 |
| Black Snake Blues | (VOC 1112) | 4/27/27 | 35.00 |
| Farewell Blues | (VOC 1152) | 11/18/27 | 35.00 |
| Tin Roof Blues | (VOC 1189) | 6/11/28 | 35.00 |
| Lazy Mama | (VOC 1190) | 6/11/28 | 35.00 |
| Got Everything | (BRN 4028) | 8/13/28 | 15.00 |
| Aunt Hagar's Blues | (VOC 1225) | 9/10/28 | 35.00 |
| Slow and Steady | (BRN 4469) | 11/14/28 | 15.00 |
| West End Blues | (VIC V-38034) | 1/16/29 | 10.00 |
| I'm Lonesome, Sweetheart | (VIC 23029) | 11/06/29 | 10.00 |
| Struggle Buggy | (VIC 23001) | 5/22/30 | 10.00 |
| Stingaree Blues | (VIC 23009) | 9/10/30 | 10.00 |
| Nelson Stomp | (VIC 23388) | 9/19/30 | 8.00 |

**OLSEN, GEORGE** NMP (.0-.50)

**OSBORNE, WILL** NMP (.0-.50)

**OWENS, HARRY** NMP (.0-.25)

# P

**PAIGE, RAYMOND** NMP (.0-.50)

**PANCHO** NMP (.0-.25)

**PASTOR, TONY** NMP (.0-1.00)

**PEERLESS QUARTET** NMP (.0-.20)

**PENDARVIS, PAUL** NMP (.0-.50)

**PICKENS SISTERS** NMP (.0-.75)

**PIPERS, PIED** NMP (.0-.50)

**POLLACK, BEN** and his various groups
  Generally NMP but for the following items:

When I First Met Mary
  (Miller, Goodman) (VIC 20394) 12/09/26 5.00

169

**Will Osborne**          Photograph courtesy Alf Hildman, West Des Moines

**Ben Pollack**          Photograph courtesy Alf Hildman, West Des Moines

**Tony Pastor**                    Photograph courtesy Alf Hildman, West Des Moines

| | | | |
|---|---|---|---|
| 'Deed I Do (Miller, Goodman) | (VIC 20408) | 12/17/26 | $ 4.00 |
| You're the One for Me (as above) | (VIC 20461) | 12/17/26 | 4.00 |
| He's the Last Word (as above) | (VIC 20425) | 12/17/26 | 4.00 |
| Memphis Blues (as above) | (VIC 21184) | 12/07/27 | 4.00 |
| Sweet Sue — Just You (as above) | (VIC 21437) | 4/26/28 | 4.00 |
| Forever (Goodman, Teagarden) | (VIC 21716) | 10/01/28 | 4.00 |
| Then Came the Dawn (as above) | (VIC 21827) | 12/03/28 | 4.00 |
| Futuristic Rhythm (as above) | (VIC 21858) | 12/24/28 | 4.00 |
| Wang-Wang Blues (Miller, Goodman, Bauduc) | (VIC 21971) | 1/22/29 | 4.00 |
| Sing-Song Girl (Spivak, Goodman, Teagarden) | (BAN 32074) | 1/21/31 | 3.50 |
| I'm a Ding Dong Daddy (as above) | (BAN 32105) | 2/12/31 | 4.00 |
| Song of the Islands (H. James, Spivak, Miller) | (BRN 7764) | 9/15/36 | 4.00 |

**POWELL, DICK**            NMP (.0-1.25)

**POWELL, TEDDY**            NMP (.0-.75)

**PRIMA, LOUIS** and his various groups
    Generally NMP but for early discs such as:

| | | | |
|---|---|---|---|
| Jamaica Shout (Brunies, Thornhill) | (BRN 7524) | 9/27/34 | 4.00 |
| Star Dust (as above) | (BRN 7335) | 9/27/34 | 4.00 |
| The Lady in Red (P.W. Russell) | (BRN 7448) | 5/17/35 | 4.00 |
| Chinatown, My Chinatown (as above) | (BRN 7456) | 5/17/35 | 4.00 |
| Darktown Strutters' Ball (as above) | (BRN 7657) | 2/28/36 | 4.00 |
| Dinah (as above) | (BRN 7666) | 2/28/36 | 4.00 |
| Sing, Sing, Sing (as above) | (BRN 7628) | 2/28/36 | 4.00 |

**PRINCE'S ORCHESTRA**            NMP (.0-2.50)

**PRYOR, ARTHUR**            NMP (.0-.20)

**PRYOR, ROGER**            NMP (.0-.25)

# *INTERMISSION 7*

## They Sold a Million: 1919-1947

In 1972 *American Pie,* a single 45 rpm disc made by Don McLean, sold 4.5 million copies. The following year Tony Orlando and Dawn's *Tie a Yellow Ribbon 'Round the Ole Oak Tree* sold in excess of 5.5 million. Clearly, the luster of the "gold record" award, originated formally in 1942 to recognize the sale of one million copies of a given disc, had been diminished by a dull patina. Besides, LP albums were breaking the "gold" barrier with astonishing regularity beginning in the early 1960s. The situation was out of hand, if not totally incomprehensible. Between 1903 and 1947 only 126 records had sold a million each. In 1969 alone (and again in 1971 and 1972) 139 discs reached that plane. Of the estimated 3,100 records qualified as "gold" since Caruso's *Vesti La Giubba* (1903), over 2,000 were released between 1961 and 1979. That fact speaks for itself.

In 1976 the R.I.A.A. (Recording Industry Association of America) adapted to the boom by promulgating fresh standards:

**Platinum Award:** To be validated as worthy of platinum status a single record (issued after New Year's Day, 1976) must sell at least two million copies (which four discs did that very first year). An LP is designated platinum when its sales attain one million. In 1976 there were 37 such awards given. By 1978 the number was up to 102.

**Gold Award:** To attain gold status a single record still has to sell one million copies. Subsequent to January 1, 1975, any LP that reached 500,000 in unit sales qualified for a gold award. In 1978 over 190 albums earned that distinction.

Although the signs for the first half of 1979 suggest that the recording industry bonanza is tapering off to a more realistic plateau the amount of copies sold each year still benumbs the imagination. Even the encomium "platinum" has lost real meaning within an industry that flirts with a yearly sales income of 4 billion dollars.

In this Intermission we shall return briefly to a time when one million sales (not to mention one million dollars) was sufficient to impress us beyond belief. Although being purchased one million times or more may not enhance a 78 rpm record's marketplace value, it does afford that disc a special place in the history of popular music. Perhaps you would like to know which of your records reached such an exalted position.

You may be surprised to notice that some of the presumed "biggies" of the period do not appear on the list. There may be a number of reasons for that discrepancy: (1) My list may not be absolutely definitive; (2) In the folklore of 78's a given record's reputation as a "classic" often exceeds its actual sales; (3) The "gold record" tradition, and the sales-boosting hoopla that surrounded such an award, did not gather momentum until the late 1930s. A fair number of popular discs released before 1940, then, failed to reach the heights because the "gold record" concept had not sunk into the public consciousness; (4) The relationship between the Depression and record sales may not be direct, but it is worth noting that as the nation moved toward solvency, the number of yearly million sellers increased steadily. There was one between 1932 and 1935. By 1942 there were forty-nine.

The material below is taken from Joseph Murrell's *Book of Golden Discs* (Barrie and Jenkins; London; 1978), a comprehensive (1903-77), invaluable reference work on which I have relied for many things. I have taken the liberty to correct a few minor chronological errors in Murrell's text and, assuming that some of us look at an artist's name on a record label before any other feature, I have organized this honor roll alphabetically by performer(s) rather than (as Murrell did) by year of release. Only "popular" 78's, meaning those made by "pop" singers and/or dance bands, are included. Certain Country and Western discs appear because of the renewed interest in older C&W 78's (which may bring up to $50 each on the current market).

That this roster of 150 millionaires terminates with 1947 is a reflection of my view that the 78 rpm record began to fade badly when the Big Bands died in the wake of World War II. Dance bands and 78's were so interwoven that one could not survive without the other for very long. Neither has managed to make a comeback.

So here you are. Twenty-nine years worth of million-sellers. The Golden 78's! How many do you still have — or have you thrown them all away?

| Artist | Record | Label/Year |
|---|---|---|
| Roy Acuff | Wabash Cannon Ball | Columbia (1942) |
| Andrews Sisters | Bei Mir Bist Du Schoen | Decca (1937) |
| | Rum and Coca Cola | Decca (1944) |
| Gene Austin | My Blue Heaven | Victor (1927) |
| | Ramona | Victor (1928) |
| Gene Autry | That Silver Haired Daddy of Mine | Columbia (1939) |
| Don Azpiazu and His Orchestra | The Peanut Vendor | Victor (1930) |
| Elton Britt | Star Bangled Banner Waving Somewhere | Victor (1942) |
| Les Brown and His Orchestra | Sentimental Journey | Columbia (1944) |
| Cab Calloway and His Orchestra | Jumpin' Jive | Columbia (1939) |
| Carmen Cavallero and His Orchestra | Chopin's Polonaise | Decca (1945) |
| Perry Como | Till the End of Time | Victor (1945) |
| | If I Loved You | Victor (1945) |
| | Dig You Later (Hubba-Hubba) | Victor (1945) |
| | Temptation | Victor (1945) |
| | Prisoner of Love | Victor (1946) |
| | I'm Always Chasing Rainbows | Victor (1946) |
| | When You Were Sweet Sixteen | Victor (1947) |
| Francis Craig and His Orchestra | Near You | Bullet (1947) |
| Bing Crosby | Sweet Leilani | Decca (1937) |
| | San Antonio Rose | Decca (1941) |
| | White Christmas | Decca (1942) |
| | Silent Night | Decca (1942) |
| | I'll Be Home for Christmas | Decca (1943) |
| | Sunday, Monday or Always | Decca (1943) |
| | Pistol Packin' Mama | Decca (1943) |
| | Jingle Bells | Decca (1943) |

| Artist | Record | Label/Year |
|---|---|---|
| | Swingin' on a Star | Decca (1944) |
| | Too-Ra-Loo-Ra-Loo-Ra | Decca (1944) |
| | Don't Fence Me In | Decca (1944) |
| | I Can't Begin to Tell You | Decca (1945) |
| | McNamara's Band | Decca (1946) |
| | South America, Take It Away | Decca (1946) |
| | Alexander's Ragtime Band | Decca (1946) |
| | Whiffenpoof Song | Decca (1947) |
| Doris Day (with Buddy Clark) | Confess | Columbia (1947) |
| Al Dexter | Pistol Packin' Mama | Okeh (1943) |
| Jimmy Dorsey and His Orchestra | Amapola | Decca (1941) |
| | Green Eyes | Decca (1941) |
| | Maria Elena | Decca (1941) |
| | Besame Mucho | Decca (1943) |
| Tommy Dorsey and His Orchestra | Marie | Victor (1937) |
| | Boogie Woogie | Victor (1938) |
| | There Are Such Things | Victor (1942) |
| | Opus No. 1 | Victor (1944) |
| | On the Sunny Side of the Street | Victor (1944) |
| Billy Eckstine | Cottage for Sale | National (1945) |
| | Prisoner of Love | National (1945) |
| | Everything I Have Is Yours | MGM (1947) |
| Ella Fitzgerald (with Ink Spots) | Into Each Life Some Rain Must Fall | Decca (1944) |
| Judy Garland | Over the Rainbow | Decca (1939) |
| Will Glahe and His Orchestra | Beer Barrel Polka | Victor (1938) |
| Arthur Godfrey | Too Fat Polka | Columbia (1947) |
| Benny Goodman and His Orchestra | Why Don't You Do Right? | Columbia (1942) |
| The Harmonicats | Peg O' My Heart | Vitacoustic (1947) |
| Coleman Hawkins | Body and Soul | Bluebird (1939) |
| Dick Haymes | You'll Never Know | Decca (1943) |
| Horace Heidt and His Orchestra | Deep in the Heart of Texas | Columbia (1941) |
| Woody Herman and His Orchestra | Woodchopper's Ball | Decca (1939) |
| | Laura | Columbia (1945) |

| Artist | Record | Label/Year |
|---|---|---|
| Eddie Heywood and His Orchestra | Begin the Beguine | Decca (1944) |
| Eddy Howard and His Orchestra | To Each His Own | Majestic (1946) |
| Ink Spots | To Each His Own | Decca (1946) |
|  | The Gypsy | Decca (1946) |
| Harry James and His Orchestra | Ciribiribin | Columbia (1939) |
|  | One O'clock Jump | Columbia (1939) |
|  | You Made Me Love You | Columbia (1941) |
|  | I Had the Craziest Dream | Columbia (1942) |
|  | Easter Parade | Columbia (1942) |
|  | I've Heard That Song Before | Columbia (1942) |
| Gordon Jenkins and His Orchestra | Maybe You'll Be There | Decca (1947) |
| Al Jolson | There's a Rainbow 'Round My Shoulder | Brunswick (1928) |
|  | April Showers | Decca (1946) |
|  | Rockabye Your Baby | Decca (1946) |
|  | You Made Me Love You | Decca (1946) |
|  | Sonny Boy | Decca (1946) |
|  | Anniversary Song | Decca (1946) |
| Isham Jones and His Orchestra | Wabash Blues | Brunswick (1921) |
| Spike Jones and His Orchestra | Der Fuehrer's Face | Bluebird (1942) |
|  | Cocktails for Two | Victor (1944) |
|  | Glow-Worm | Victor (1946) |
| Louis Jordan and His Tympany Five | Is You Is or Is You Ain't? | Decca (1943) |
|  | Caldonia Boogie | Decca (1945) |
|  | Choo Choo Ch' Boogie | Decca (1946) |
| Stan Kenton and His Orchestra | Artistry in Rhythm | Capitol (1943) |
|  | Tampico | Capitol (1945) |
|  | Shoo-Fly Pie | Capitol (1945) |
| Kay Kyser and His Orchestra | Three Little Fishies | Brunswick (1939) |
|  | Praise the Lord and Pass the Ammunition | Columbia (1942) |
|  | Strip Polka | Columbia (1942) |
|  | Who Wouldn't Love You? | Columbia (1942) |
|  | Jingle Jangle Jingle | Columbia (1942) |
| Frankie Laine | That's My Desire | Mercury (1947) |

| Artist | Record | Label/Year |
|---|---|---|
| Art Landry and His Orchestra | Dreamy Melody | Gennett (1923) |
| Guy Lombardo and His Orchestra | Humoresque | Decca (1946) |
| | Christmas Island | Decca (1946) |
| | Easter Parade | Decca (1947) |
| Johnny Long and His Orchestra | Shanty in Old Shanty Town | Decca (1940) |
| Art Lund | Mam'selle | Decca (1947) |
| Freddy Martin and His Orchestra | Piano Concerto No. 1 | Bluebird (1941) |
| | White Christmas | Victor (1942) |
| Tony Martin | To Each His Own | Mercury (1946) |
| Clyde McCoy and His Orchestra | Sugar Blues | Decca (1935) |
| Glenn Miller and His Orchestra | Little Brown Jug | Bluebird (1939) |
| | Moonlight Serenade | Bluebird (1939) |
| | In the Mood | Bluebird (1939) |
| | Pennsylvania 6-5000 | Bluebird (1940) |
| | Tuxedo Junction | Bluebird (1940) |
| | Chattanooga Choo Choo | Bluebird (1941) |
| | Kalamazoo | Victor (1942) |
| | American Patrol | Victor (1942) |
| Mills Brothers | Tiger Rag | Brunswick (1931) |
| | Paper Doll | Decca (1942) |
| | You Always Hurt the One You Love | Decca (1944) |
| Vaughn Monroe and His Orchestra | Racing with the Moon | Bluebird (1941) |
| | There, I've Said It Again | Victor (1945) |
| | Ballerina | Victor (1947) |
| Art Mooney and His Orchestra | I'm Looking over a Four Leaf Clover | MGM (1947) |
| Red Nichols and His Five Pennies | Ida, Sweet as Apple Cider | Okeh (1927) |
| Ray Noble and His Orchestra | By the Light of the Silvery Moon | Columbia (1941) |
| George Olsen and His Orchestra | Who? | Victor (1925) |
| Pied Pipers | Dream | Capitol (1944) |
| Jimmie Rodgers | Blue Yodel | Victor (1928) |
| | Brakeman's Blues | Victor (1928) |

| Artist | Record | Label/Year |
|---|---|---|
| David Rose and His Orchestra | Holiday for Strings | Victor (1944) |
| Ben Selvin and His Orchestra | Dardanella | Victor (1919) |
| Artie Shaw and His Orchestra | Begin the Beguine | Bluebird (1938) |
| | Nightmare | Bluebird (1938) |
| | Back Bay Shuffle | Bluebird (1938) |
| | Traffic Jam | Bluebird (1939) |
| | Frenesi | Victor (1940) |
| | Stardust | Victor (1940) |
| | Summit Ridge Drive | Victor (1940) |
| | Dancing in the Dark | Victor (1941) |
| Dinah Shore | Blues in the Night | Victor (1941) |
| Frank Sinatra (with Harry James) | All or Nothing at All | Columbia (1939) |
| | White Christmas | Columbia (1944) |
| Freddie Slack and His Orchestra | Cow-Cow Boogie | Capitol (1943) |
| Kate Smith | Rose O'Day | Columbia (1941) |
| Orrin Tucker and His Orchestra | Oh, Johnny, Oh | Columbia (1939) |
| Ernest Tubb | Walkin' the Floor over You | Decca (1941) |
| Chick Webb and His Orchestra | A-Tisket, A-Tasket | Decca (1938) |
| Ted Weems and His Orchestra | Piccolo Pete | Victor (1929) |
| | Heartaches | Victor (1933) |
| | Mickey | Decca (1947) |
| Paul Whiteman and His Orchestra | Whispering | Victor (1920) |
| | Three O'clock in the Morning | Victor (1922) |
| | Linger Awhile | Victor (1923) |
| Margaret Whiting | Moonlight in Vermont | Capitol (1944) |
| Bob Wills and His Texas Playboys | San Antonio Rose | Okeh (1940) |

By way of a final footnote to this section, I should mention that between 1903 and 1947 only six records in the Classical/Semiclassical category attained sales of one million each, all released on the VIC label it so happened. They were:

| | |
|---|---|
| Boston "Pops" Orchestra | *Jalousie* (1938) |
| Enrico Caruso | *Vesti La Giubba* (1903) |
| Nelson Eddy and Jeanette MacDonald | *Indian Love Call* (1936) |
| Alma Gluck | *Carry Me Back to Old Virginny* (1915) |
| Jose Iturbi | *Polonaise in A Flat* (1945) |
| Philadelphia Symphony (Stowkowski) | *Tales from the Vienna Woods* (1939) |

(Perhaps you have heard that the *Guinness Book of World Records* came forth in October, 1979 with a new way of recognizing super sales. To composer-artist Paul McCartney the Guiness establishment awarded a "Rhodium Record", made from the rare compound, rhodium. Gold and platinum have been thus topped as the standard forms by which superlative success may be measured. Whether or not a trend has been initiated remains to be seen).

**Teddy Powell**          Photograph courtesy Alf Hildman, West Des Moines

# R

**RADIOLITES, THE**                 NMP (.0-.50)

**RAEBURN, BOYD**                    NMP (.0-1.00)

**RANDALL, CLARK** and his orchestra

| | | | |
|---|---|---|---|
| Troublesome Trumpet | | | |
| (Spivak, Miller, Matlock) | (BRN 7415) | 3/15/35 | $ 3.50 |
| Jitterbug (as above) | (BRN 7466) | 3/22/35 | 3.50 |
| Drifting Tide (as above) | (BRN 7436) | 3/29/35 | 3.50 |

**RAVAZZA, CARL**                    NMP (.0-.25)

**RAY, JIMMY**                       NMP (.0-.25)

**REGA ORCHESTRA**                   NMP (.0-.20)

**REGAN, PHIL**                      NMP (.0-.25)

**REGENT CLUB ORCHESTRA**            NMP (.0-.20)

**REICHMAN, JOE**                    NMP (.0-.50)

**REISMAN, LEO** and his orchestra
Generally NMP with these borderline exceptions:

| | | | |
|---|---|---|---|
| Body and Soul (Bubber Miley) | (VIC 22537) | 9/19/30 | 3.50 |
| I Love Louisa (F. Astaire) | (VIC 22755) | 6/30/31 | 3.50 |
| Hoops (Fred and Adele Astaire) | (VIC 22836) | 10/19/31 | 3.50 |
| A Rainy Day (Clifton Webb) | (VIC 24157) | 10/05/32 | 3.00 |
| Night and Day (F. Astaire) | (VIC 24193) | 11/22/32 | 3.00 |
| The Gold Diggers' Song | | | |
| (as above) | (VIC 24315) | 5/02/33 | 2.50 |
| Easter Parade (Clifton Webb) | (VIC 24418) | 10/03/33 | 2.50 |

**RENARD, JACQUES**                  NMP (.0-.20)

**REVELERS, THE**                    NMP (.0-1.25)

**REY, ALVINO**
Generally NMP but for these few sides:

| | | | |
|---|---|---|---|
| Tiger Rag (King Sisters) | (BLB 11002) | 11/18/40 | 2.50 |
| Nighty-Night (theme) | (BLB 11041) | 2/03/41 | 2.50 |

| | | | |
|---|---|---|---|
| William Tell Overture (2 pts.) | (BLB 11072) | 2/03/41 | $ 2.50 |
| Light Cavalry | (BLB 11108) | 3/28/41 | 2.50 |
| Hindustan | (BLB 11136) | 4/14/41 | 2.50 |
| Hall of the Mountain King | (BLB 11216) | 6/10/41 | 2.50 |
| Jealous | (BLB 11272) | 7/14/41 | 2.00 |
| Liebestraum | (BLB 11404) | 11/25/41 | 2.00 |
| The Major and the Minor | (BLB 11573) | 7/24/42 | 2.00 |

**REYNOLDS, TOMMY**                NMP (.0-.50)

**RICH, FRED** and his orchestra
  Generally NMP but for these recordings:

| | | | |
|---|---|---|---|
| Bell Hoppin' Blues | | | |
| (Bauduc, Mole) | (HAR 119H) | 2/02/26 | 2.50 |
| Drifting and Dreaming | | | |
| (T. Dorsey) | (PAT 36389) | 2/03/26 | 2.50 |
| Christina (Dorseys) | (PAT 36980) | 5/29 | 2.50 |
| Dixie Jamboree | | | |
| (Berigan, Dorseys) | (COL 2043D) | 11/15/29 | 2.00 |

**RILEY-FARLEY ORCHESTRA**

| | | | |
|---|---|---|---|
| Music Goes 'Round and Around | (DEC 578) | 10/24/35 | 3.50 |

**RINES, JOE**                NMP (.0-.20)

**RING, JUSTIN**

| | | | |
|---|---|---|---|
| True Blue Lou (Dorseys) | (OKE 41295) | 8/16/29 | 2.50 |

**ROBERTSON, DICK** and his orchestra
  Generally NMP except these four discs:

| | | | |
|---|---|---|---|
| Louise (Nichols, Miller) | (BRN 4367) | 4/29 | 4.00 |
| Ho Hum! (Dorseys) | (MEL 12162) | 5/01/31 | 4.00 |
| Bull Fiddle Blues | | | |
| (J. Dorsey, Venuti) | (MEL 12418) | 6/07/32 | 4.00 |
| West Bound Freight (as above) | (MEL 12417) | 6/07/32 | 4.00 |

**ROBESON, PAUL**                TIP

| | | | |
|---|---|---|---|
| Water Boy | (VIC 19824) | 1/07/26 | 3.00 |

| | | | |
|---|---|---|---|
| Deep River | (VIC 20793) | 5/10/27 | $ 3.00 |
| Ol' Man River (P. Whiteman) | (VIC 35912) | 3/01/28 | 4.00 |
| Ballad for Americans (4 pts.) | (VIC 26516,17) | 2/09/40 | 5.00 |

## ROBINSON, BILL "BOJANGLES"

| | | | |
|---|---|---|---|
| Doin' the New Low-Down | (BRN 4535) | 9/11/29 | 4.00 |
| Just a Crazy Song | (BRN 6134) | 5/27/31 | 4.00 |
| Doin' the New Low-Down (Redman) | (BRN 6520) | 12/29/32 | 4.00 |

## RODIN, GIL and his orchestra

| | | | |
|---|---|---|---|
| Beale Street Blues (Spivak, Teagarden) | (CRN 3017) | 9/30 | 4.00 |
| If I Could Be with You (as above) | (CRN 3016) | 9/30 | 4.00 |
| Ninety-Nine Out of a Hundred (Goodman) | (CRN 3045) | 9/30 | 4.50 |
| Hello, Beautiful! (Goodman, Bauduc, Matlock) | (CRN 3046) | 9/30 | 4.50 |

## ROGERS, CHARLES "BUDDY"    NMP (.0-.50)

## ROGERS, GINGER

| | | | |
|---|---|---|---|
| Isn't This a Lovely Day? | (DEC F-5746) | 8/25/35 | 8.00 |
| Cheek to Cheek | (DEC F-5747) | 8/25/35 | 8.00 |
| Eeny, Meeny, Miney Mo (J. Mercer) | (DEC 638) | 11/27/35 | 6.00 |
| Let Yourself Go (J. Dorsey) | (DEC F-5963) | 4/03/36 | 7.50 |
| The Yam | (BLB 7981) | 10/06/38 | 5.00 |

## ROLFE, B.A.    NMP (.0-.75)

## ROLLINI, ADRIAN and his orchestra

| | | | |
|---|---|---|---|
| Have You Ever Been Lonely? (Dorseys, Venuti) | (BAN 32698) | 2/14/33 | 5.00 |
| You've Got Me Cryin' Again (as above) | (BAN 32699) | 2/14/33 | 5.00 |
| Blue Prelude (Goodman, Dorseys) | (COL 2785D) | 6/12/33 | 5.00 |

**Buddy Rogers**    Photograph courtesy Alf Hildman, West Des Moines

Ah! But Is It Love?

| | | | |
|---|---|---|---|
| (P.W. Russell, Berigan) | (BAN 32826) | 7/29/33 | $ 5.00 |
| Dream On (as above) | (BAN 32827) | 7/29/33 | 5.00 |
| By a Waterfall (as above) | (BAN 32867) | 9/14/33 | 4.00 |
| I'll Be Faithful | (MEL 12790) | 9/14/33 | 5.50 |

And So, Goodbye

| | | | |
|---|---|---|---|
| (Berigan, Goodman) | (BAN 32873) | 10/16/33 | 4.00 |
| Savage Serenade (as above) | (BAN 32880) | 10/16/33 | 4.00 |

Get Goin'

| | | | |
|---|---|---|---|
| (J. Dorsey, Barnet, Krupa) | (BRN 6786) | 2/26/34 | 4.50 |

Butterfingers

| | | | |
|---|---|---|---|
| (Goodman, Berigan) | (VOC 2672) | 3/24/34 | 4.50 |
| Sugar (Goodman, Teagarden) | (DEC 265) | 10/23/34 | 5.00 |
| Davenport Blues (as above) | (DEC 359) | 10/23/34 | 5.00 |

**ROLLINS, TODD**  NMP (.0-.25)

**ROSE, DAVID**  NMP (.0-.50)

**ROSS, LANNY**  NMP (.0-.50)

**RUSSELL, ANDY**  NMP (.0-.50)

**RUSSO-FIO RITO ORIOLE
   ORCHESTRA**  NMP (.0-.25)

# S

**SAMUELS, JOSEPH**  NMP (.0-.20)

**SANDERS, JOE**  NMP (.0-.20)

**SAVITT, JAN** and his orchestra
   Generally NMP not including these items:

| | | | |
|---|---|---|---|
| Futuristic Shuffle | (BLB 7733) | 7/22/38 | 3.50 |
| Quaker City Jazz (theme) | (BLB 10005) | 10/21/38 | 3.50 |
| 720 in the Books | (DEC 2771) | 9/23/39 | 3.50 |
| Sugar Foot Strut | (VIC 27464) | 5/05/41 | 3.00 |

**SCHUBERT, ADRIAN**  NMP (.0-.20)

## SCHUTT, ARTHUR

| | | | |
|---|---|---|---|
| My Fate Is in Your Hands (Dorseys) | (OKE 41346) | 11/18/29 | $ 4.00 |
| Take Everything but You (as above) | (OKE 41345) | 11/18/29 | 4.00 |
| I'm Following You! (as above) | (OKE 41360) | 12/04/30 | 4.00 |
| Have a Little Faith in Me (as above) | (OKE 41359) | 1/04/30 | 4.00 |
| Montana Call (as above) | (OKE 41391) | 3/04/30 | 4.00 |

**SCOTT, HAZEL**          NMP (.0-.50)

**SCOTT, RAYMOND**          NMP (.0-.50)

**SELVIN, BEN**          NMP (.0-.50)

**SENTER, BOYD** and his various groups

| | | | |
|---|---|---|---|
| Mobile Blues | (PAR 20341) | 6/24 | 7.00 |
| Fat Mama Blues | (PAR 20364) | 10/24 | 6.00 |
| Craving | (PAT 36270) | 5/01/25 | 6.00 |
| Slippery Elm | (PAT 36256) | 5/01/25 | 6.00 |
| Bucktown Blues | (PAT 36285) | 5/01/25 | 6.00 |
| St. Louis Blues | (PAT 36397) | 11/13/25 | 6.00 |
| I Wish I Could Shimmy . . . (Dorseys) | (OKE 41018) | 3/23/28 | 6.00 |
| Original Chinese Blues (Dorseys) | (OKE 41163) | 5/08/28 | 6.00 |
| Wabash Blues (Dorseys, P. Napoleon) | (VIC 21864) | 1/30/29 | 5.00 |
| Shine (Dorseys, E. Lang) | (VIC 21912) | 3/13/29 | 5.00 |

**SHAND, TERRY**          NMP (.0-.50)

**SHAW, ARTIE\*** and his orchestra

\*I confess to some distress when it comes to pricing Shaw records. For the most part his discs hover in the $2-3 range, and there are far too many of those to list here. His BRN and VOC recordings (1936-37) are rather rare but seem to generate no widespread concern beyond the $5 level. His efforts on VIC (1940-45) and MUS

(1946) are miniclassics but cannot seem to break the $3.50 barrier. This perturbs me some only because I am partial to his work, which is a sentiment that changes the value of his records not one whit. Herewith I list a selected cluster of Shaw records because I simply cannot pass him over without noting a few of his imperishable discs.

| | | | |
|---|---|---|---|
| Begin the Beguine | (BLB 7746) | 7/24/38 | $ 3.50 |
| Any Old Time | | | |
| (Billie Holiday vocal) | (BLB 7759) | 7/24/38 | 4.00 |
| Nightmare (theme) | (BLB 7875) | 9/27/38 | 4.00 |
| Copenhagen | (BLB 10054) | 11/17/38 | 3.00 |
| One Night Stand | (BLB 10202) | 3/17/39 | 3.00 |
| Traffic Jam | (BLB 10385) | 6/12/39 | 3.00 |
| Frenesi | (VIC 26542) | 3/03/40 | 3.00 |
| Special Delivery Stomp | (VIC 26762) | 9/03/40 | 3.00 |
| Summit Ridge Drive | (VIC 26763) | 9/03/40 | 3.00 |
| Star Dust | (VIC 27230) | 10/07/40 | 3.00 |
| Blues (2 pts.) | (VIC 27411) | 12/04/30 | 2.50 |
| Concerto for Clarinet (12″, 2 pts.) | (VIC 36383) | 12/17/40 | 4.00 |
| Moonglow | (VIC 27405) | 1/23/41 | 3.00 |
| St. James' Infirmary (2 pts.) | (VIC 27895) | 11/12/41 | 2.50 |
| 'S Wonderful | (VIC 20-1638) | 1/09/45 | 2.50 |
| September Song | (VIC 20-1668) | 4/05/45 | 2.50 |
| In the Still of the Night | (MUS 390) | 6/23/46 | 2.00 |

**SHERWOOD, BOBBY** and his orchestra

The Elks Parade (CAP 107) 5/05/42 $ 2.50

**SHILKRET, JACK** NMP (.0-.20)

**SHILKRET, NAT** NMP (.0-.25)

**SHORE, DINAH** NMP (.0-1.00)

**SINATRA, FRANK** NMP (.0-1.25)

**SISSLE, NOBLE** and his various groups

| | | | |
|---|---|---|---|
| Broadway Blues (with Eubie Blake) | (EMR 10296) | 7/20 | 7.50 |
| Crazy Blues (as above) | (EMR 10326) | 12/20 | 7.50 |
| Crazy Blues (as above) | (EDI 50754) | 1/11/21 | 6.00 |
| Boo Hoo Hoo (as above) | (EMR 15012) | 1/04/22 | 6.00 |
| Waitin' for the Evenin' Mail (as above) | (VIC 19086) | 5/25/23 | 6.00 |
| Dixie Moon (as above) | (VIC 19464) | 10/22/24 | 5.00 |
| Broken Busted Blues (as above) | (EDI 51572) | 6/10/25 | 6.00 |

**SLACK, FREDDIE** NMP (.0-.50)

| | | | |
|---|---|---|---|
| **SMECK, ROY** | NMP (.0-.20) | | |
| **SMITH, ETHEL** | NMP (.0-.20) | | |
| **SMITH, JOSEPH C.** | NMP (.0-.20) | | |

**SMITH, KATE**
Generally NMP except for these few recordings:

| | | | |
|---|---|---|---|
| One Sweet Letter from You | | | |
|   (Red Nichols) | (COL 911D) | 2/14/27 | $ 8.00 |
| When the Moon Comes over | | | |
|   the Mountain | (COL 2516D) | 8/17/31 | 7.50 |
| Too Late (Guy Lombardo) | (COL 2578D) | 12/08/31 | 7.50 |
| God Bless America | (VIC 26198) | 3/21/39 | 6.00 |

| | | | |
|---|---|---|---|
| **SOSNIK, HARRY** | NMP (.0-.10) | | |

**SPANIER, MUGGSY** and his Ragtime Band

| | | | |
|---|---|---|---|
| Big Butter and Egg Man (Brunies) | (BLB 10417) | 7/07/39 | 3.50 |
| That Da Da Strain (Brunies) | (BLB 10384) | 7/07/39 | 3.50 |
| At the Jazz Band Ball | | | |
|   (Brunies, Bushkin) | (BLB 10518) | 11/10/39 | 3.50 |
| Dippermouth Blues (as above) | (BLB 10506) | 11/10/39 | 3.50 |
| Riverboat Shuffle (as above) | (BLB 10532) | 11/22/39 | 3.50 |
| At Sundown | (BLB 10719) | 11/22/39 | 3.50 |
| Lonesome Road | (BLB 10766) | 12/12/39 | 3.50 |
| Dinah | (BLB 10682) | 12/02/39 | 3.50 |

| | |
|---|---|
| **SPECHT, PAUL** | NMP (.0-.75) |
| **SPITALNY, PHIL** | NMP (.0-.25) |
| **SPIVAK, CHARLIE** | NMP (.0-1.00) |
| **STABILE, DICK** | NMP (.0-1.00) |
| **STAFFORD, JO** | NMP (.0-.50) |
| **STEELE, BLUE** | NMP (.0-1.00) |
| **STRAETER, TED** | NMP (.0-.25) |
| **SULLIVAN, MAXINE** | NMP (.0-.50) |

# INTERMISSION 8

## *Bye-Bye, 78's — a Memoir*

In the summer of 1948 I was halfway through Amherst College and taking enrichment courses across town at the University of Massachusetts. To bolster my spirits I brought a liberal sampling of my 78 rpm records from home to my quarters in a near-vacant fraternity house. I began buying 78's in 1943 (with tips earned from bellhopping) and I felt I had a handsome collection. They were my pride and joy, my relief from absolute silence, my sole ties to the innocent days before Pearl Harbor.

It was a period of contradictory emotions. The Olympiad promised much excitement. News that Babe Ruth would not survive his battle with cancer saddened us. Through it all I found solace in my 78's. The Dorseys, Stan Kenton, Artie Shaw, Glenn Miller (gone from us less than four years then), Kay Kyser — they kept me company as I labored through the humid summer.

I had heard that my heroes were laboring too. The big band business was in the doldrums, the experts said, and the future was anything but clear. The record ban of 1948 was doing less damage than its predecessor had during the late war but, somehow, the old buoyancy was missing. A number of important bands dissolved after 1945. Some regrouped but there was uncertainty in the ranks. You could read it between the lines in *Down Beat*. I was not overly concerned, of course. Amherst, Massachusetts, was at least a light year away from commercial centers where such issues were being debated, and, anyway, I had my trusty 78's to pacify me. When in doubt, put a 10″ tranquilizer on the turntable.

I had no idea their days were numbered. If a soothsayer had approached me and whispered: "Beware the Ides of June. Within a decade 78 rpm records will be no more" — like Caesar I would have pushed the man aside and continued on my path. You know what befell Caesar.

While I was pursuing my studies a new age in recording was dawning.

Commercially the industry appeared to be in good health. Over 400 million records and 3.4 million phonographs were sold in 1947 (up from 275 million records in 1946). But the disc record itself had not advanced in either appearance or composition as far as it should have since 1901. In 1947, after three years of intensive experimentation, a major company came forward with a magnetic tape that could record sounds at 15,000 cycles at a speed of 7.5" per second. That was the first serious assault on the supremacy of the 78. The second blow proved fatal, and it was delivered while I was in class one day in June, 1948.

The notion that disc records could be constructed to deliver more than three minutes of music per side was not peculiar to the 1940s. In 1905 Neophone developed 20" long-playing records. Twenty years thereafter Brunswick-Balke-Collender unveiled a 12" disc that offered forty minutes (both sides, total) at 78 rpm, a feat refined by Thomas Edison in 1927. Had the economic climate been better and courage more abundant, RCA could have shattered the pyschic barrier in the early 1930s. RCA developed a 33⅓ rpm transcription-like disc for home use but failed to seek closure on related aspects such as inexpensive, adaptable machines, disc quality, and tonal excellence. This new product made a faltering debut in New York on September 17, 1931. When no groundswell of professional interest was forthcoming RCA shelved the idea, which might well have revived the moribund record industry in 1932-1933.

While the record-phonograph-radio-jukebox business was enjoying an upswing in the late 1930s, Budapest native Peter C. Goldmark became a U.S. citizen (1937). Seven years later he was leading a laboratory task force of CBS-Columbia Records technicians toward the production of a prototype "practical slow-speed micro-groove record," with positive results. On June 21, 1948, the "revolutionary" Columbia LP was introduced at a New York press conference. Goldmark (1906-1977) would make more contributions to the communications field but none more spectacular and influential. The LP transmogrified the entire record world, as we see now in retrospect.

Caught somewhat off-guard, RCA Victor nevertheless counterattacked with the 7", 45 rpm disc (and special player) in February, 1949, and what became known as the "battle of the speeds" was underway. Columbia took round one, of course. The LP was so widely welcomed that within six months it was a resounding success aesthetically and financially. Round two went to Columbia as well. In late 1949 Capitol and Decca adopted the LP mode, leaving Victor (and its weaker ally, Capitol) with the problem of selling the 45 rpm concept to a perplexed public. RCA ate crow and capitulated to the LP in January, 1950. The fight was not over however. The 45 began to gather strength in 1950 and Victor took round three when Columbia opted to produce 45's in February, 1951, in order to remain competitive at the "pop" music level. By 1954 more than 200 million 45's had been purchased. The "speed war" ended in a draw, actually. A delighted public was able to make room for both 45's and 33⅓'s in their lives and all parties seemed pleased that the record market had stabilized by 1952-1953. The Victor-Columbia war went on — over price cuts, record clubs, stereo, quadraphonics — for another twenty years, but the record buyer has been in seventh heaven all the while.

Meanwhile, back in Amherst, I was oblivious to most of the transitional events of 1948-1950. Certainly the 78 rpm record was destined to continue, I thought. Smooth, shiny, high fidelity 78's were still being released by Tommy Dorsey, Ralph Flanagan, Sauter-Finegan, Nat Cole, Jo Stafford, Ray Anthony, and Buddy Clark, were they not? Why worry? As fate often has it, the Korean War took me out of circulation and when I returned from overseas in June, 1952, (just four years after Goldmark's announcement) the world had changed. LP's and 45's were everywhere. Phonographs had been altered to accommodate the two new speeds. By 1954 the 45 took over the "pop" field and 78's were receding noticeably. Five years later it was all over. I was now the owner of a modest collection of curiosity pieces. This year a teenager asked me: "What is a 78?" Ugh.

I did not realize it at the time but while I was taking courses that distant summer of 1948 the 78 rpm record was fading into obsolescence. Come to think of it, so was I — and I did not realize that either. *Sic transit gloria mundi,* fellow 78 rpm record lovers.

**Johnny "Scat" Davis** and **Gloria Van**
Photograph courtesy Alf Hildman, West Des Moines

# T

**TEAGARDEN, JACK** and his orchestra
Generally NMP but for these possible exceptions:

| | | | |
|---|---|---|---|
| Loveless Love (Goodman) | (CRN 3051) | 1/31 | $ 8.00 |
| You Rascal, You | | | |
|   (F. Waller, P.W. Russell) | (COL 2558D) | 10/14/31 | 8.00 |
| Lies (Matlock, Bauduc, Rodin) | (BAN 32325) | 11/10/31 | 7.50 |
| Stars Fell on Alabama | | | |
|   (Goodman, Trumbauer) | (BRN 6993) | 9/18/34 | 6.00 |

**THORNHILL, CLAUDE**      NMP (.0-1.00)

**THREE SUNS, THE**      NMP (.0-.75)

**TODD, DICK**      NMP (.0-.50)

**TRACE, AL**      NMP (.0-.20)

**TROTTER, JOHN SCOTT**      NMP (.0-.50)

**TROUBADOURS, THE**      NMP (.0-.50)

**TRUMBAUER, FRANKIE** and his orchestra

| | | | |
|---|---|---|---|
| Clarinet Marmalade | | | |
|   (Bix, J. Dorsey) | (OKE 40772) | 2/04/27 | 10.00 |
| Riverboat Shuffle (Bix) | (OKE 40822) | 5/09/27 | 8.00 |
| 'Way Down Yonder in New | | | |
|   Orleans (Bix) | (OKE 40843) | 5/13/27 | 10.00 |
| Blue River (Bix, E. Lang) | (OKE 40879) | 8/25/27 | 8.00 |
| Wringin' and Twistin' (Bix, Lang) | (OKE 40916) | 9/17/27 | 15.00 |
| Krazy Kat (Bix, Venuti, Lang) | (OKE 40903) | 9/28/27 | 10.00 |
| Baltimore (as above) | (OKE 40926) | 9/28/27 | 10.00 |
| Jubilee (Bix, J. Dorsey, Malneck) | (OKE 41044) | 1/09/28 | 10.00 |
| Mississippi Mud (Bing Crosby) | (OKE 40979) | 1/20/28 | 10.00 |
| My Pet (Bix, Lang, Malneck) | (OKE 41039) | 4/10/28 | 8.00 |
| Raisin' the Roof (as above) | (OKE 41209) | 3/08/29 | 7.50 |
| I Like That (as above) | (OKE 41286) | 4/30/29 | 7.50 |
| Blue Moon | | | |
|   (Shaw, Miller, Berigan) | (VIC 24812) | 11/20/34 | 7.50 |
| 'S Wonderful (Shaw, Teagarden) | (BRN 7663) | 4/27/36 | 6.00 |

**Frank Trumbauer**　　　　Photograph courtesy Alf Hildman, West Des Moines

To all
from
Bonnie Baker

**Bonnie Baker featured with Orrin Tucker**
Photograph courtesy Alf Hildman, West Des Moines

**TUCKER, ORRIN**                    NMP (.0-.50)

**TUCKER, SOPHIE**

After You've Gone
  (Mole, J. Dorsey, Nichols)   (OKE 40837)   4/11/27 $ 8.00
Some of These Days       (VIC 22049)   7/10/29  10.00

**TUCKER, TOMMY**                    NMP (.0-1.00)

**TUXEDO ORCHESTRA**                 NMP (.0-.20)

# U

**UNIVERSITY ORCHESTRA** (directed by Sam Lanin)

Button Up Your Overcoat
  (T. Dorsey, Venuti, Lang)   (GEN 6815)   4/01/29  8.00
I've Got a Feeling I'm Fallin
  (as above)          (GEN 6862)   5/23/29  8.00
Am I Blue? (as above)    (GEN 6892)   6/27/29  8.00
Ain't Misbehavin' (as above) (GEN 6966)   8/27/29  8.00
When the Real Thing Comes
  Along (as above)     (GEN 7028)  10/14/29  8.00
Why Was I Born? (as above) (GEN 7042)  11/21/29  8.00
Happy Days Are Here Again
  (Teagarden)       (GEN 7117)   2/10/30  7.00
Gone (T. Dorsey)      (GEN 7172)   3/07/30  7.00
Swingin' in a Hammock
  (Teagarden)       (GEN 7234)   7/18/30  6.00
I'm Yours (T. Dorsey)   (GEN 7277)   8/26/30  6.00

# V

**VALLEE, RUDY** and his orchestra
  Clearly NMP with these modest exceptions:
Deep Night          (VIC 21868)   2/06/29  2.50
My Time Is Your Time (theme) (VIC 21924)   2/25/29  3.00

**Rudy Vallee**

| | | | |
|---|---|---|---|
| I'm Just a Vagabond Lover | (VIC 21967) | 4/01/29 | $ 3.00 |
| Heigh-Ho! Everybody, | | | |
| Heigh-Ho! | (VIC 22029) | 6/03/29 | 2.50 |
| Stein Song | (VIC 22321) | 2/10/30 | 2.50 |
| Kitty from Kansas City | (VIC 22419) | 4/30/30 | 2.50 |
| Betty Co-Ed | (VIC 22473) | 6/25/30 | 2.50 |
| As Time Goes By | (VIC 22773) | 7/25/31 | 3.00 |
| The Drunkard Song | (VIC 24721) | 9/07/34 | 2.50 |

**VENUTI, JOE** and his various groups

| | | | |
|---|---|---|---|
| I Must Be Dreaming | (OKE 41051) | 5/25/28 | 8.00 |
| Pickin' Cotton (J. Dorsey) | (OKE 41087) | 7/24/28 | 8.00 |
| Doin' Things (Dorseys, Lang) | (OKE 41113) | 10/04/28 | 8.00 |
| Weary River (as above) | (OKE 41192) | 2/02/29 | 7.00 |
| Out of Breath (as above) | (OKE 41451) | 9/06/30 | 7.00 |
| Wasting My Love on You | | | |
| (Miller, J. Dorsey) | (VIC 23018) | 9/30/30 | 7.00 |
| Doin' the Uptown Lowdown | | | |
| (J. Dorsey) | (BAN 32874) | 9/25/33 | 6.00 |
| Fiddlesticks | (BLB 5293) | 10/13/33 | 5.00 |
| Everybody Shuffle | (BLB 5520) | 10/13/33 | 5.00 |

**VORHEES, DON**                    NMP (.0-.50)

# W

**WALD, JERRY**                    NMP (.0-.50)

**WALDORF ASTORIA ORCHESTRA** NMP (.0-.10)

**WALLER, THOMAS "FATS"***

and his various groups                    TIP

| | | | |
|---|---|---|---|
| Muscle Shoals Blues (solo) | (OKE 4757) | 10/21/22 | 10.00 |
| St. Louis Blues (organ solo) | (VIC 20357) | 11/17/26 | 10.00 |
| Soothin' Syrup Stomp | (VIC 20470) | 1/14/27 | 9.00 |
| Messin' Around with the Blues | (VIC 20655) | 1/14/27 | 9.00 |
| Rusty Pail | (VIC 20492) | 1/14/27 | 9.00 |

| | | | |
|---|---|---|---|
| Hog Maw Stomp (piano) | (VIC 21525) | 2/16/27 | $ 9.00 |
| Beale Street Blues | (VIC 20890) | 5/20/27 | 9.00 |
| Sugar (Alberta Hunter vocal) | (VIC 20771) | 5/20/27 | 25.00 |
| Fats Waller Stomp | (VIC 20890) | 5/20/27 | 9.00 |
| Savannah Blues | (VIC 20776) | 5/20/27 | 9.00 |
| The Minor Drag | (VIC 38050) | 3/01/29 | 9.00 |
| Ain't Misbehavin' (piano) | (VIC 22092) | 8/02/29 | 9.00 |
| Valentine Stomp | (VIC 38554) | 8/02/29 | 8.00 |
| Smashing Thirds | (VIC 38613) | 9/24/29 | 8.00 |
| Lookin' Good . . . (H. Allen, Teagarden, Krupa) | (VIC 38086) | 9/30/29 | 10.00 |
| Ridin' but Walkin' (Allen, Teagarden) | (VIC 38119) | 12/18/29 | 8.00 |
| St. Louis Blues (with Bennie Paine) | (VIC 22371) | 3/21/30 | 9.00 |

*From 1931-42 Waller made scores of sides for VIC and BLB. My judgment is that they fall into the $2.50-5.00 range generally, with the earlier records bringing the higher prices.

**WARING, FRED**                      NMP (.0-.50)

**WARNOW, MARK**                      NMP (.0-.25)

**WEBB, CHICK**

As a rule NMP, but these few might be deserving:

| | | | |
|---|---|---|---|
| Heebie Jeebies | (VOC 1607) | 3/30/31 | 5.00 |
| Sunny Side of the Street | (COL 2875D) | 12/20/33 | 4.00 |
| Darktown Strutters' Ball | (COL CB-754) | 1/15/34 | 4.00 |
| I Can't Dance | (COL 2920D) | 5/09/34 | 3.50 |
| Stomping at the Savoy | (COL 2926D) | 5/18/34 | 3.50 |
| Blue Minor | (OKE 41572) | 7/06/34 | 3.50 |
| Don't Be That Way | (DEC 483) | 11/19/34 | 3.00 |
| I'll Chase the Blues Away (Ella Fitzgerald) | (BRN 02602) | 6/12/35 | 3.50 |
| A-Tisket, A-Tasket (as above) | (DEC 1840) | 5/02/38 | 2.50 |

**WEBER, MAREK**                      NMP (.0-.50)

Photographs courtesy RCA Victor

**Dolly Mitchell vocalist with Paul Whiteman**

Photograph courtesy Alf Hildman, West Des Moines

To. "Alf"
Every good wish
From the
M
S

**Lawrence Welk**          Photograph courtesy Alf Hildman, West Des Moines

## WEEKS, ANSON                    NMP (.0-.50)

**WEEMS, TED** and his orchestra
NMP invariably, except these very few curiosities:

| | | | |
|---|---|---|---|
| Heartaches | (BLB 5131) | 8/04/33 | $ 5.00 |
| That Old Gang of Mine (Perry Como vocal) | (DEC 2829) | 10/04/39 | 3.00 |
| I Wonder Who's Kissing Her Now (Como) | (DEC 2919) | 10/05/39 | 3.00 |
| May I Never Love Again (Como) | (DEC 3627) | 1/27/41 | 3.00 |
| Out of the Night (theme) | (DEC 3697) | 1/27/41 | 3.50 |

**WELK, LAWRENCE** and his orchestra
Usually NMP, with the following allowances:

| | | | |
|---|---|---|---|
| Spiked Beer | (GEN 6712) | 11/16/28 | 10.00 |
| Shanghai Honeymoon | (GEN 20341) | 11/16/28 | 10.00 |
| Doin' the New Low Down | (GEN 6697) | 11/17/28 | 10.00 |
| Smile, Darn Ya, Smile | (BWY 1462) | 5/31 | 8.00 |
| Beer Barrel Polka | (VOC 4788) | 4/02/39 | 3.50 |
| Clarinet Polka | (DEC 3726) | 3/26/41 | 2.50 |
| Pennsylvania Polka | (DEC 4309) | 3/03/42 | 2.50 |

## WHITE, LEW                      NMP (.0-.25)

**WHITEMAN, PAUL** and his orchestra

| | | | |
|---|---|---|---|
| Whispering | (VIC 18690) | 8/23/20 | 2.50 |
| Rhapsody in Blue (12″, 2 pts.) (G. Gershwin) | (VIC 55225) | 6/10/24 | 10.00 |
| Muddy Water (Bing Crosby) | (VIC 20508) | 3/07/27 | 5.00 |
| Rhapsody in Blue (12″, 2 pts.) (G. Gershwin) | (VIC 35822) | 4/21/27 | 8.00 |
| When Day Is Done (12″) (H. Busse) | (VIC 35828) | 6/08/27 | 4.00 |
| Whiteman Stomp (Dorseys, Busse) | (VIC 21119) | 8/11/27 | 4.00 |
| Mississippi Suite (12″, 2 pts.) | (VIC 35859) | 9/07/27 | 4.00 |

**Ted Weems**　　　　　Photograph courtesy Alf Hildman, West Des Moines

**Paul Whiteman**    Photograph courtesy Alf Hildman, West Des Moines

| | | | |
|---|---|---|---|
| Washboard Blues | | | |
| (Bix, Dorseys, Carmichael) | (VIC 35877) | 11/18/27 | $ 5.00 |
| Changes (Bix, Dorseys, | | | |
| Crosby, Busse) | (VIC 21103) | 11/23/27 | 5.00 |
| Ol' Man River (Crosby) | (VIC 21218) | 1/11/28 | 8.00 |
| Ol' Man River (P. Robeson) | (VIC 35912) | 3/01/28 | 4.00 |
| Concerto in F (6 pts.) | (COL 50139 | | |
| | etc.) | 9/15/28 | 5.00 |
| | | | |
| Grand Canyon Suite | | | |
| (multiple parts) | (COL 36052 | | |
| | etc.) | 4/26/32 | 5.00 |
| | | | |
| A Night with Paul Whiteman at | | | |
| the Biltmore (12″) | (VIC 39000) | 12/02/32 | 4.00 |
| Park Avenue Fantasy (12″) | (VIC 36131) | 9/11/34 | 4.00 |
| Anything Goes — Medley (12″) | (VIC 36141) | 10/26/34 | 3.50 |
| Top Hat — Medley (12″) | (VIC 36175) | 9/28/35 | 3.50 |
| Slaughter on Tenth Avenue | | | |
| (2 pts.) (12″) | (VIC 36183) | 6/26/36 | 3.50 |
| The General Jumped at Dawn | (CAP 101) | 4/42 | 3.50 |
| Serenade in Blue | (CAP 108) | 4/42 | 3.00 |
| Travelin' Light (Billie Holiday) | (CAP 116) | 6/12/42 | 4.00 |
| The Old Music Master | | | |
| (Mercer, Teagarden) | (CAP 137) | 6/12/42 | 3.00 |

**WHITING, MARGARET**            NMP (.0-1.00)

**WILLIAMS, BERT**

| | | | |
|---|---|---|---|
| Nobody | (COL A-1289) | 1/07/13 | 5.00 |

**WILLIAMS, CLARENCE** and his various groups

| | | | |
|---|---|---|---|
| Pullman Porter Blues | (OKE 8020) | 10/11/21 | 7.50 |
| Roumania | (OKE 8021) | 10/11/21 | 7.50 |
| Brown Skin | (OKE 8027) | 12/05/21 | 15.00 |
| Weary Blues (piano solo) | (OKE 4893) | 5/23 | 7.50 |
| Wild Cat Blues (Bechet) | (OKE 4925) | 7/30/23 | 50.00 |
| Achin' Hearted Blues | (OKE 4966) | 8/27/23 | 50.00 |
| New Orleans Hop Scop Blues | (OKE 4975) | 10/03/23 | 50.00 |

| | | | |
|---|---|---|---|
| Oh Daddy! Blues | (OKE 4993) | 10/03/23 | $ 50.00 |
| Shreveport | (OKE 40006) | 11/10/23 | 50.00 |
| Texas Moaner Blues | | | |
|   (Louis Armstrong) | (OKE 8171) | 10/17/24 | 50.00 |
| Everybody Loves My Baby | | | |
|   (as above) | (OKE 8181) | 11/06/24 | 50.00 |
| Mandy, Make Up Your Mind | | | |
|   (as above) | (OKE 40260) | 12/17/24 | 50.00 |
| Cake-Walking Babies From Home | | | |
|   (as above) | (OKE 40321) | 1/08/25 | 50.00 |
| Pickin' on Your Baby (as above) | (OKE 40330) | 1/08/25 | 40.00 |
| Papa Da-Da-Da | | | |
|   (Armstrong, Redman) | (OKE 8215) | 3/04/25 | 45.00 |
| Livin' High Sometimes | (OKE 8272) | 10/06/25 | 45.00 |
| Santa Claus Blues | (OKE 8254) | 10/16/25 | 45.00 |
| You Can't Shush Kate | | | |
|   (C. Hawkins, Armstrong) | (OKE 8342) | 10/26/25 | 35.00 |
| Shake That Thing | (OKE 8267) | 12/15/25 | 45.00 |
| I've Found a New Baby | | | |
|   (Redman, B. Miley) | (OKE 8286) | 1/22/26 | 30.00 |
| Would Ja? (Ladnier, Hawkins) | (OKE 8443) | 12/10/26 | 15.00 |
| Shut Your Mouth (F. Waller) | (PAR 12435) | 1/27 | 10.00 |
| Gravier Street Blues (B. Moten) | (COL 14193D) | 1/25/27 | 8.00 |
| Candy Lips (Moten) | (OKE 8440) | 1/29/27 | 8.00 |
| Cushion Foot Stomp | (OKE 8462) | 4/13/27 | 10.00 |
| Black Snake Blues | (OKE 8465) | 4/14/27 | 20.00 |
| Slow River | (BRN 3580) | 6/07/27 | 7.00 * |
| Bottomland | (PAR 12517) | 7/27 | 7.00 |
| Close Fit Blues | (OKE 8510) | 9/23/27 | 20.00 |
| Yama Yama Blues | (OKE 8525) | 11/25/27 | 20.00 |
| Red River Blues (K. Oliver) | (OKE 8584) | 5/23/28 | 10.00 |
| Lazy Mama (as above) | (OKE 8592) | 6/23/28 | 15.00 |
| Farm Hand Papa | | | |
|   (James P. Johnson) | (COL 14341D) | 7/20/28 | 10.00 |
| Long Deep and Wide | (QRS 7004) | 8/28 | 25.00 |

| | | | |
|---|---|---|---|
| Squeeze Me | (QRS 7005) | 8/28 | $ 25.00 |
| Organ Grinder Blues | (OKE 8617) | 9/20/28 | 15.00 |
| Walk That Broad | | | |
|   (Claude Hopkins) | (OKE 8629) | 9/26/28 | 10.00 |
| Wildflower Rag (K. Oliver) | (QRS 7003) | 11/28 | 25.00 |
| Longshoreman's Blues (as above) | (QRS 7040) | 11/28 | 10.00 |
| In the Bottle Blues (as above) | (OKE 8645) | 11/23/28 | 20.00 |
| Sister Kate (as above) | (QRS 7044) | 12/28 | 25.00 |
| Saturday Night Jag | (PAR 12870) | 1/29 | 20.00 |
| You Don't Understand | | | |
|   (J.P. Johnson) | (OKE 8752) | 11/19/29 | 10.00 |
| I've Found a New Baby (as above) | (COL 14502D) | 1/31/30 | 10.00 |
| He Wouldn't Stop Doin' It | | | |
|   (I. Robinson) | (OKE 8798) | 5/22/30 | 25.00 |

**WILLIAMS, GRIFF**  NMP (.0-.50)

**WILLSON, MEREDITH**  NMP (.0-.50)

**WILSON, TEDDY** and his orchestra

| | | | |
|---|---|---|---|
| I Wished on the Moon | | | |
|   (Goodman, B. Holiday) | (BRN 7501) | 7/02/35 | 5.00 |
| What a Little Moonlight Can Do | | | |
|   (as above) | (BRN 7498) | 7/02/35 | 5.00 |
| Sweet Lorraine | | | |
|   (Eldridge, Kirby, C. Cole) | (BRN 7520) | 7/31/35 | 4.00 |
| Rosetta (piano solo) | (BRN 7563) | 10/07/35 | 6.00 |
| On Treasure Island (as above) | (BRN 7572) | 11/22/35 | 6.00 |
| Breaking in a Pair of Shoes | | | |
|   (as above) | (BRN 7599) | 1/17/36 | 6.00 |
| My Melancholy Baby | | | |
|   (E. Fitzgerald) | (BRN 7729) | 3/17/36 | 5.00 |
| You Came to My Rescue | | | |
|   (Goodman, Krupa, Hampton) | (BRN 7739) | 8/24/36 | 5.00 |
| Easy to Love | | | |
|   (Holiday, Musso, Krupa) | (BRN 7762) | 10/21/36 | 5.00 |

**Bob Zurke**　　　　　　　　Photograph courtesy Alf Hildman, West Des Moines

| | | | |
|---|---|---|---|
| Pennies from Heaven (Holiday, Goodman, J. Jones) | (BRN 7789) | 11/19/36 | $ 5.00 |
| Why Was I Born? (Holiday, Goodman) | (BRN 7859) | 1/25/37 | 5.00 |
| I'll Get By (Holiday, Hodges, L. Young) | (BRN 7903) | 5/11/37 | 5.00 |
| You're My Desire (H. James, Goodman, Krupa) | (BRN 7940) | 7/30/37 | 5.00 |
| Don't Blame Me (piano solo) | (BRN 8025) | 11/12/37 | 5.00 |
| April in My Heart (Holiday, James, Carter) | (BRN 8265) | 11/09/38 | 5.00 |
| They Say (as above) | (BRN 8270) | 11/09/38 | 5.00 |
| What Shall I Say? (Carter, Holiday, Eldridge) | (BRN 8314) | 1/30/39 | 4.00 |

**WOOD, BARRY**      NMP (.0-.25)

# Y

**YERKES, HARRY A.**      NMP (.0-.10)

**YOUNG, VICTOR**      NMP (.0-.50)

# Z

**ZOLLO, LEO**      NMP (.0-.25)

**ZURKE, BOB**      NMP (.0-2.50)

# INTERMISSION 9

## *What Now, Big Bands?*

A substantial portion of the 78's people collect, trade, or discover in their attics were made during the decade 1935-45, the so-called "Big Band Era." My price guide tells you something about the relative value of those discs but nothing of the story that runs in counterpoint to the economic factor. During this brief intermission we will consider the past, present, and future of the big band scenario. Of course I leave to you any final judgments you might wish to cast as to what will happen next in the tricky world of pop music.

The nostalgia movement spilled over in the early 1970s into the mental compartment we reserve for the big bands, and they bobbed to the surface once again. Actually, the big band pilot light never was extinguished totally, but it flickered faintly from 1955 to 1965 for two reasons: obsolescence and competition (from other musical forms). A combination of events, among them the publication of George Simon's *The Big Bands* (Macmillan; New York; 1967), and Reader's Digest's spate of boxed LPs such as "In the Groove" and "The Great Band Era," heralded a new drift toward the big band mode. Once that notion got caught in the web of nostalgia being spun from coast to coast it was only a matter of time until the artifacts of the 1935-45 period attained a fresh significance.

Before we proceed I should differentiate between the two major tributaries on which big bandism floats: the Olde Big Band syndrome, which draws sustenance from a restoration mentality; and the Neo-Big Band strain, which bears but a peripheral connection to the nostalgia fever of the 1970s.

The Neo category is populated (sparsely) by musicians who find no nourishment in nostalgia and have pushed the big band style far beyond the redundancies of the thirties and forties (toward true ensemble jazz). Foremost illustrations of this creativity may be found in the Thad Jones-Mel Lewis group and the Toshiko Akiyoshi/Lew Tabackin Big Band. Also, there is a cluster of personalities from the Olde period who strive to change with the times and are outspokenly anti-nostalgic:

Woody Herman, Count Basie, Stan Kenton, Buddy Rich, for example. They refuse to replicate *ad nauseam* the musty arrangements of the Olde Daze and put as much distance between themselves and that exhausted idiom as they can. A few quotes make the point: Herman ("I can hardly bear the whole nostalgia scene."); Harry James ("Really, it's so ridiculous to try and go back."); Rich ("There is no such thing as the good old days."). During the 1970s Artie Shaw, Tommy Tucker, and the late Vaughn Monroe made similar pronouncements from retirement. So much for the camp that disdains the temptation to woo the public into a musical coma.

The Olde Big Band forces are more numerous and better blessed with mass media coverage. Many radio stations employ disc jockeys who spin "classics" from 1935-45 and purr about the swing era. Magazines *(Liberty; Nostalgia Illustrated; The Complete History of the Big Bands)* take us on periodic safaris through the favored decade. Even *TV Guide* (March 18, 1978) published a paeon to those "glorious years" of the Olde orchestras. Any one who haunts shopping malls knows that since 1970 the number of LPs devoted to vintage band recordings (Lunceford, Hall, Bryant, Shaw, Miller, Dorseys, Himber, Ellington, Savitt, Thornhill, to cite a handful) have multiplied like weeds. It is not uncommon to read in album notes assertions such as "Big bands are as alive and well in the seventies as ever!" (which is patently false, if one uses 1935-45 as a reference point).

Unlike the Neo-phytes who "struck a compromise with time" there are those who appear to believe that (a) the Olde era will be reconstituted, and (b) while we are waiting, there is no harm in serving the public's need to re-experience the past. Abe Most, Charlie Barnet, Ray McKinley, the peripatetic "Glenn Miller" orchestras, and the Society for the Preservation of Big Bands sixteen-member unit would be gathered, with others, under the reactionary umbrella. They have in common the wistful conviction that 1935 is just around the musical bend (again) and the wisdom to recognize a sound financial venture.

The "mild resurgence" in the big band business *Time* magazine forecast (November 18, 1966) never matured, in part because it was sucked into the nostalgia movement and deprived of some of its vitality.

Public attention was diverted from the Neo to the Olde. Since the past is known and the future is obscure, many of us opt for what we think we remember.

Where does the issue stand today? One thing is clear at least: their records may be in vogue but the Olde Big Bands have not "come back." In fact, the Neo-phytes have not truly arrived. They continue to beep around the core of popular music like distant satellites. Will there be another big band era of the compelling magnitude we witnessed between 1935 and 1945? Most thoughtful observers have responded to that question with a flat "never." For such a redivivus to occur, they contend, a number of unlikely variables would have to coalesce, namely: (a) there would have to be a strong public demand for big bands; (b) places for them to perform would have to be available; (c) certain economic and social conditions would have to prevail; and (d) the big bands would have to have something special to say musically. No coalition, no revival.

Four years ago I would have said "amen" and joined the skeptics. Today I am not so sure. I see in the Disco movement the seeds of a big band return. As the *New York Times* pointed out (December 17, 1978) Disco has moved beyond faddism to become a "national nightly pastime." What are its salient characteristics? Couples going out together at night; a focus on dancing to "big" musical (often 1940-based) arrangements; a return to prominence of ballroom-size emporiums; participation by people of all social classes and ages. Sound reminiscent of the late 1930s? Two elements remain to be altered and we will have the makings of a second big band era: the anonymity of the Disco jockey is replaced by live orchestras, and societal pressures provoke a togetherness comparable to that of the 1935-45 period. A big band dimension may turn out to be the logical zone for Disco to modulate into after this phase flames out.

Save your cactus needles, boys — the big band may rise again! [1]

[1] I must add to this speculation several supporting comments. During the summer of 1978 Harry James made some remarks apropos to the possible Disco-to-Big Band modulation. Noting that our youth was

being re-introduced to tunes from the swing era in Disco parlors James said: "People are very much interested in older songs because they've found out they're very adaptable to disco dancing." Adaptation could well phase into transformation, in time. And in a convincing piece in *New Times* (January 8, 1979), "Disco Tech," Andrew Kopkind informs us that Disco is both "here to stay" and likely to spread its influence more deeply and broadly in the years ahead. "Disco music may have only minor merit as melody, but it makes a major metaphor for the sensibility of the generation," Kopkind observed. Readers who wish to contemplate upon this notion further might consult: Kitty Hanson, *Disco Fever* (Signet; New York; 1978); *Disco World* (March, 1979), 2; "Disco Takes Over," *Newsweek* (April 2, 1979), 56-64; and the entire issue of *Rolling Stone* (April 19, 1979).

---

**NOTE:** It is not uncommon to find at flea markets, secondhand stores, and in one's own attic numbers of three- or four-record 78 rpm albums. They vary in value of course but you may use a very simple rule of thumb: such an album is worth the sum total of the records inside, assuming they are in excellent condition and in proper numerical sequence. For example, a four-disc album by Paul Weston (CAP BD37, "Music For Memories") would be priced at $2.50-3, given the low esteem in which Weston 78's are held. A Duke Ellington album of four records (COL C-38, "Hot Jazz Classics") on the other hand might be worth $6-10. (So little because the records inside are reissues from the early 1930s on BRN.) The condition of the storage album itself can add or detract $1-1.50 to the total price of the unit.

# PART TWO

# Classical Records (1900-1940)

In this section I will report briefly and straightforwardly on the marketability of old 78 rpm classical records. This is a very active, complex specialization that attracts a good deal of attention from dealers, collectors and general citizens alike. I cannot do this subject justice in the space set aside for it in this *Guide*, of course. But neither can I ignore the classical market entirely in this volume as I did in my previous *Guide*. As a compromise I offer this spare, alphabetized appendix. Perhaps it will fill the existing void until a more ambitious researcher prepares a comprehensive index of the worthy old classical recordings of the stature of Julian M. Moses', *Price Guide to Collectors' Records* (American Record Collectors' Exchange; New York; 1967), on which I relied heavily for inspiration.

Let me remind you that no records are cited here which are valued at *less* than $3, which, perforce, eliminates many of the discs you have stored in your attic. You may therefore assume that whatever you own that does *not* appear here falls within the 0.-2.50 range. Furthermore, because of this exclusion, you will not find a number of artists you might have expected to see (e.g. Nelson Eddy, Grace Moore, Gladys Swarthout, Lawrence Tibbett, James Melton, several orchestras of note). The cold fact is that most of the classical records, and multi-disc albums, you have access to are not extremely valuable. May I say also that in my listings I do not differentiate between (1) discs recorded in Europe and imported into our market on domestic labels, of which there were very many between 1903 and 1907, and discs cut *in* the U.S.A., and (2) single-sided and double-sided records.

My methodology in arriving at prices is simple. I took Moses' figures as a base reference point and adjusted them by applying two modifiers, (1) my own observations of sale prices garnered over the past five years, and (2) contemporary price ranges presented in auction lists and other documents circulated by professional dealerships such as Rondo, Ltd., Immortal Performances, and Mr. Records. As is usual, my recommendations are as open to debate as anyone's. This is only a beginning. I hope it will help you evaluate what you have in the way of classical remnants.

# A

ABOTT, Bessie (sop.)

Red seal VIC records (1907-08) in the 87000-89000 numbering series: $4-10.

ACKTE, Aino (sop.)

1903 VIC red seal sides 5068, 5072, 5074 may be assessed at $10-15.

ADAMS, Suzanne (sop.)

Very uncommon sides for COL in the 1190 series rated at $30. About one-half of that for VIC red seals in the 5000 series. All recorded circa 1903.

AFFRE, Augustarello (ten.)

Several VIC red seals (5073, 5076) imported in 1903: $5-7.

AGUSSOL, Charlotte (sop.)

VIC red seal 5076 from 1903: $8.

ALBANI, Carlo (ten.)

1908 VIC red seals in the 64000, 74000 sequences: $8.

ALDA, Frances (sop.)

VIC red seals of the 87000-88000 series (1910-12) run from $4-10. About $3-5 for those in 64000, 74000 series (1923-24).

ALTHOUSE, Paul (ten.)

VIC red seal number 76031 (1915): $7.

AMATO, Pasquale (bar.)

Pre-WWI VIC red seals in 87000-89000 (or 6000-8000) series: $4-10. Several COL discs (48922, 48944) from 1917: $5.

ANCONA, Mario (bar.)

1907-09 VIC red seals in 87000-89000 series: $7-10.

ANSSEAU, Fernand (ten.)

VIC red seals in the 74000 and 6000 series: $3.

ARIMONDI, Vittorio (bass)

COL sides in the 30000 (or A 5000) sequence: $9-12.

ARRAL, Blanche (sop.)     1909 VIC red seals (64000, 74000 series): $4-8.

AUSTRAL, Florence (sop.)     VIC red seal (8063) from 1925: $7.

# B

BAKLANOFF, George (bar.)     Early (1911) COL discs in the A 5000 grouping: $4-5.

BARRIENTOS, Maria (sop.)     For her COL sides with "D", "M" suffixes (1916-20): $3.

BATTISTINI, Mattia (bar.)     VIC red seals from 1903 in 5000 series: $10-15. Later VIC sides in 80000 and 90000 groupings fall between $5-8.

BEDDOE, Daniel (ten.)     $3-5 for his 64000 series on VIC red seal (1911-14).

BELLATTI, Virgilio (bar.)     Bare $3 for COL sides (A 5076) made in 1908.

BERTANA, Luisa (mez.-sop.)     VIC red seals 6483, 6485 (1925) at about $6.

BESANZONI, Gabriella (cont.)     VIC red seals in 64000, 74000 clusters: $3-7.

| | |
|---|---|
| BISPHAM, David (bar.) | COL (1906-10) in early A 5000 series: $4-9. Tapers off to $3 by A 5600's (1915). |
| BLANCHART, Ramon (bar.) | Modest $3 for COL sides in 30000 and A 5100-A 5200 series (1910-11). |
| BLASS, Robert (bass) | VIC red seals in series 64000, 74000, 81000, and 85000: $5-12. |
| BLAUVELT, Lillian (sop.) | VIC red seals (on 81000, 85000 series) made in 1905: $5-12. 1907-09 COL sides in A 5000 series: $8-12. |
| BOHNEN, Michael (bar.-bass) | BRN sides in 15000, 50000 sequences: $3-4. |
| BONCI, Alessandro (ten.) | COL records (1913) in A 5400 series: $5-7. |
| BONINSEGNA, Celestina (sop.) | Red seal VIC discs (1907-10) of the 88000, 90000 series: $5-8. COL sides (A 5000 and 5000M): $6-7. |
| BORI, Lucrezia (sop.) | VIC red seals in 87000, 88000 groups $3-7; later VICs down below $3. |
| BORONAT, Olimpia (sop.) | VIC 88242 (1910) about $7. |
| BRASLAU, Sophie (cont.) | Barely $3 for VIC red seals of 64000 and 6000 series. |
| BRONSKAJA, Eugenie (sop.) | Weak $3 for A 5000 series COL sides (ca. 1910). |
| BROZIA, Zina (sop.) | A 1242, A 5417 COL sides (1912-13): $5-8. |
| BURZIO, Eugenia (sop.) | COL discs with "H" prefixes (1911-13): $6-9. |
| BUTT, Clara (cont.) | 88000 series VIC red seals (1912-13): $3-4. |

# C

CALVE, Emma (sop.) — 1903 VIC red seals in 5000 series: $12-20. Sides in 88000, 91000 sequences $3-10. Drops off to $5-7 for 6000 series (1907-16).

CAMPAGNOLA, Leon (ten.) — VIC red seals 64251, 74297 (1912) from $4-7.

CAMPANARI, Giuseppe (bar.) — 1903 COL sides 1224-27, 1445 a strong $25-30. VIC red seals in 80000 series off a bit to $7-12.

CARUSO, Enrico (ten.) — VIC red seals (1903) in the 5000 series may be assayed at $10-25. Later discs in the 81000 and 85000 series drop off to $7-10. From 1910-20 Caruso discs float in the $4-6 zone. Slightly more for records on which other renown artists join him in duets, sextets, etc.

CASTELLANO, Edoardo (ten.) — COL sides of the 30000 and A 5000 series range from $5-9.

CAVALIERI, Elda (sop.) — VIC red seals of the 64000, 74000 sequences (1906-7) fall into the $5-9 range.

CAVALIERI, Lina (sop.) — 1910-13 COL records (30000, A 5100 series): $3-7.

CHALIAPIN, Feodor (bass) — Red seal VIC records 88461, 88462 (1914) $5. Others in the 88000, 6000 series about $3.

CHAMLEE, Mario (ten.) — BRN discs (1920-25) in 15000, 50000 series: $3-4.

CLEMENT, Edmond (ten.) — 1912-13 VIC red seals in the 64000, 74000, and 76000 series: $3-7.

CONSTANTINO, Florencio (ten.) — A few COL sides from the A 5100, A 5200 series (1909-10) may bring $4-6.

| | |
|---|---|
| CRIMI, Giulio (ten.) | Some selected VOC issues made between 1920-24 in the 52000, 55000, 60000, 70000 groupings might reach $3. |
| CROSSLEY, Ada (cont.) | 1903 VIC red seals numbered 2186-91 rare at $35. Later issues of same in 81000 series: $10. |
| CULP, Julia (cont.) | WWI vintage VIC red seals in the 64000, 74000, and 6000 brackets: $3-6. |

# D

| | |
|---|---|
| DAL MONTE, Toti (sop.) | VIC red seals of the 1100, 6400 series (1924-25): $4-6. |
| DALMORES, Charles (ten.) | 81000-95000 series on VIC red seal from $4-8. |
| DANISE, Giuseppe (bar.) | Sides for BRN fall in $3-4 range for 50000, 15000 series. |
| DE CASAS, Bianca (cont.) | VIC red seals of 87000, 88000 series (1910-11): $3-5. |
| DE CISNEROS, Eleonora (cont.) | A few of her 1915 COL sides (A 56000 series): $10. |

| | |
|---|---|
| DELMAS, Jean F. (bar.-bass) | 1903 VIC red seals numbered 5077-83 approximately $10. |
| DE LUCA, Giuseppe (bar.) | VIC 1903 red seals 5039-41: $10. Remainder $3-5. |
| DE LUCIA, Fernando (ten.) | 1903 VIC red seals 5025-49 may bring $10-12. Later efforts on VIC $3-7. |
| DE LUSSAN, Zelie (mez.-sop.) | Early (1903) VIC red seals, series 2187-99, 2301 may reach $35. Same in 81000 series: $10. |
| DE PASQUALI, Bernice (sop.) | COL sides (1912-14) in A 5300, A 5500 series $4-7. |
| DE RESZKE, Edouard (bass) | 1903 COL sides 1221-23, A 617 a high $100. |
| DEREYNE, Fely (sop.) | COL disc A 1234 (1912) at $5. |
| DE SEGUROLA, Andrea (bass) | COL sides A 1214-15, S 16, H 1070 at $3-5. |
| DESMOND, Mary (cont.) | 1911 COL records (A 5256-59) might reach $3. |

| | |
|---|---|
| DESTINN, Emmy (sop.) | $7-9 for her COL sides in A 5300, A 5600 series. VIC red seals in 6000 series (1914-17) drop off to $5-7. |
| DE TURA, Gennaro (ten.) | VIC red seals in 76000, 87000-89000 series $3-7. |
| DONALDA, Pauline (sop.) | $5 for VIC red seal 87108 (1912). |
| DUFRANNE, Hector (bar.) | COL sides in A 5400 series about $5. |
| DUX, Claire (sop.) | 15000, 50000, 10100 series BRN records (1921-25): $3-5. |

# E

| | |
|---|---|
| EAMES, Emma (sop.) | VIC red seals (1905-09) of the 85000, 88000 series: $4-10, as for those in 95000 zone. |

# F

| | |
|---|---|
| FARRAR, Geraldine (sop.) | VIC red seals (1907-23) in 87000, 89000, 6000 sequences fall into $3-8 range. |
| FERRARI-FONTANA, Edoardo (ten.) | COL sides (1915) A 1731, A 5663, A 5721 verge on $10 a piece. |
| FINZI-MAGRINI, Giuseppina (sop.) | For her VIC red seal (8059) with Titta Ruffo: $7. |
| FLETA, Miguel (ten.) | $3-6 for his VIC red seals (1922-25) in the 900, 1000, 6000, and 8000 bloc. |
| FORNIA, Rita (cont.) | VIC red seals from 1911-12 in the 64000, 74000 series: $5. |
| FREEMAN, Betina (mez.-sop.) | 1910 COL sides in A 5200, A 850 series: $3-7. |
| FREMSTAD, Olive (sop.) | Early discs on COL in A 1400, A 1500, A 5200 series may be evaluated at $8-12. |

229

# *INTERMISSION* **10**

## *In Memoriam*

With each passing year we are deprived of the presences of artists who gave us much pleasure during the lifespan of the 78 rpm record. We pay them homage when we play their records. We marvel at their charismatic longevity. From the most worn discs they fairly leap out of the past and re-penetrate our imaginations. They are sorely missed. They will never return in the physical sense — but, through the repetitive courtesies of our old 78's, we may invite them back and, for just a moment, pretend they are among us still. I ask your indulgence if I have omitted your favorite from this roster of 200 immortals. Join me now in a bittersweet journey through our hall of fame.

### Popular Artists
(Dates of decease in parentheses)

Irving Aaronson (1963)
Henry "Red" Allen (1967)
Bert Ambrose (1973)
Albert Ammons (1949)
Ivy Anderson (1949)
Louis Armstrong (1971)
Gus Arnheim (1955)
Jan August (1976)
Gene Austin (1972)
Mitchell Ayres (1969)
Mildred Bailey (1971)
Phil Baker (1963)
Roy Bargy (1974)
Franklyn Baur (1950)
Nora Bayes (1928)
Sidney Bechet (1959)
Bix Beiderbecke (1931)
Bunny Berigan (1942)
Ben Bernie (1943)
Don Bestor (1970)
Earl Bostic (1965)
Connee Boswell (1976)

Al Bowlly (1941)
Tiny Bradshaw (1969)
Henry Busse (1955)
Buddy Clark (1949)
Nat "King" Cole (1965)
Russ Columbo (1934)
Zez Confrey (1972)
Charlie Cook (1956)
Carleton Coon (1932)
Jessie Crawford (1962)
Bing Crosby (1977)
Frank Crumit (1943)
Frank Dailey (1956)
Meyer Davis (1976)
Eddie DeLange (1949)
Jack Denny (1950)
Carroll Dickerson (1957)
Johnny Dodds (1940)
Sam Donahue (1974)
Jimmy Dorsey (1957)
Tommy Dorsey (1956)
Eddy Duchin (1951)

**Ray Eberle**                    Photograph courtesy Alf Hildman, West Des Moines

Ray Eberle (1979)
Duke Ellington (1974)
Ziggy Elman (1968)
Skinnay Ennis (1963)
Jim Europe (1919)
Percy Faith (1976)
Ted Fio Rito (1971)
Jan Garber (1977)
Judy Garland (1969)
Erroll Garner (1977)
Jean Goldkette (1962)
Al Goodman (1972)
Glen Gray (1963)
Jimmy Grier (1959)
Mal Hallett (1952)
W. C. Handy (1958)
Coleman Hawkins (1969)
Ted Heath (1969)
Fletcher Henderson (1952)
Art Hickman (1930)
Tiny Hill (1972)
Richard Himber (1966)
Les Hite (1962)
Johnny Hodges (1970)
Billie Holiday (1959)
Eddy Howard (1963)
Jack Jenney (1945)
Al Jolson (1950)
Isham Jones (1956)
Spike Jones (1965)
Roger Wolfe Kahn (1962)
Art Kassel (1965)
Hal Kemp (1940)
Bill Kenney (1978)
Stan Kenton (1979)
Freddie Keppard (1933)
Teddi King (1977)
Gene Krupa (1973)
Ted Lewis (1971)
Guy Lombardo (1977)
Johnny Long (1972)
Vincent Lopez (1975)
Bert Lown (1962)
Jimmie Lunceford (1947)
Abe Lyman (1957)
Enric Madriguera (1973)
Fate Marable (1947)
Johnny Marvin (1944)
Matty Matlock (1978)

Hal McIntyre (1959)
Johnny Mercer (1976)
Glenn Miller (1944)
Lucky Millinder (1966)
Carmen Miranda (1955)
Vaughn Monroe (1973)
Russ Morgan (1969)
Bennie Moten (1935)
Ozzie Nelson (1975)
Red Nichols (1965)
Ray Noble (1978)
Phil Ohman (1954)
King Oliver (1938)
George Olsen (1971)
Oran Page (1954)
Tony Pastor (1969)
Ben Pollack (1971)
Elvis Presley (1977)
Louis Prima (1978)
Boyd Raeburn (1966)
Don Redman (1963)
Joe Reichman (1970)
Leo Reisman (1961)
B.A. Rolfe (1956)
Jimmy Rushing (1972)
Luis Russell (1963)
Joe Sanders (1965)
Kenny Sargent (1969)
Jan Savitt (1948)
Noble Sissle (1975)
Freddie Slack (1965)
Muggsy Spanier (1967)
Paul Specht (1954)
Phil Spitalny (1970)
Jack Teagarden (1964)
Claude Thornhill (1965)
Alphonso Trent (1959)
John Scott Trotter (1975)
Sophie Tucker (1966)
Joe Venuti (1978)
Jerry Wald (1973)
Fats Waller (1943)
Mark Warnow (1949)
Chick Webb (1939)
Anson Weeks (1969)
Ted Weems (1963)
Paul Whiteman (1967)
Barry Wood (1970)
Bob Zurke (1944)

# Classical Artists

Frances Alda (1952)
Pasquale Amato (1942)
Elsie Baker (1958)
John Barbirolli (1970)
Thomas Beecham (1966)
E. Power Biggs (1977)
Jussi Bjoerling (1960)
Enrico Caruso (1921)
Robert Casadesus (1972)
Feodor Chaliapin (1938)
Alfred Cortot (1962)
Richard Crooks (1973)
Walter Damrosch (1950)
Emilio De Gogorza (1949)
Giuseppe De Luca (1950)
Nelson Eddy (1967)
Mischa Elman (1967)
Geraldine Farrar (1961)
Kirsten Flagstad (1962)
Amelita Galli-Curci (1963)
Mary Garden (1967)
Beniamino Gigli (1957)
Alma Gluck (1938)
Victor Herbert (1924)
Myra Hess (1965)
Louise Homer (1947)
Jan Kiepura (1966)
Serge Koussevitsky (1951)
Fritz Kriesler (1962)
Wanda Landowska (1959)

Mario Lanza (1959)
Jeanette MacDonald (1965)
Giovanni Martinelli (1969)
John McCormack (1945)
Nellie Melba (1931)
James Melton (1961)
Dimitri Mitropolous (1960)
Pierre Monteaux (1964)
Grace Moore (1947)
Charles Munch (1968)
Frank Munn (1953)
Ignace Paderewski (1941)
Ezio Pinza (1957)
Lily Pons (1976)
Fritz Reiner (1963)
Paul Robeson (1976)
Artur Rodzinski (1958)
Sigmund Romberg (1951)
Titta Ruffo (1953)
Ernestine Schumann-Heink
   (1936)
Leopold Stokowski (1977)
Gladys Swarthout (1969)
George Szell (1970)
Lawrence Tibbett (1960)
John Charles Thomas (1960)
Arturo Toscanini (1957)
Bruno Walter (1962)
Leonard Warren (1960)
Felix Weingartner (1942)

---

Sources to consult: Necrology section of annual issues of *Variety;* biographical dictionaries of musical figures; *New York Times* Obituary Index; Roger D. Kinkle, *The Complete Encyclopedia of Popular Music and Jazz: 1900-1950* (Arlington House; New Rochelle, New York; 1974), volumes 2, 3.

# G

GADSKI, Johanna (sop.)  General range $4-10 for VIC red seals numbered between 81000-89000 (1903-17).

GALEFFI, Carlo (bar.)  VIC red seals (1925) numbers 6484, 6485 at about $6.

GALLI-CURCI, Amelita (sop.)  No more than $4 for 1917-25 VIC red seal discs.

GALVANY, Maria (sop.)  $3-8 for her 87000-89000 series (1910-14) on VIC.

GARBIN, Edoardo (ten.)  VIC red seals 5037, 5038 (1903) at $10-12.

GARDEN, Mary (sop.)  1911-13 COL sides in A 1100, A 5200, A 5400 series $5-10.

GARRISON, Mabel (sop.)  Not above $3 for her 1916-20 VIC red seals in 74000 grouping.

GAUTHIER, Eva (sop.)  VIC red seal number 6151 (1921) at about $6.

GAY, Maria (cont.)  VIC disc 6407 (1908) perhaps $6. 1911-13 COL sides in A 5200-5400 series about $8.

GERVILLE-REACHE, Jeanne (cont.)  VIC red seals from 1909-12 in 80000-88000 series $5-9.

GIGLI, Beniamino (ten.)  6000 series on VIC red seal (1920-25) level off at $3-6.

GILIBERT, Charles (bar.)  Early (1903) sides for COL numbered 1234-54: $30. Later COL discs in A 5000 bloc down to $10. Sides for VIC (1907-10) in 74000, 81000, 85000, 88000, 89000 series $5-9.

GIORGINI, Aristodemo (ten.)  $3-7 for his VIC red seals in 76000, 87000-89000 series.

| | |
|---|---|
| GIRALDONI, Eugenio (bar.) | VIC red seal 5042 (1903) at about $15. |
| GLUCK, Alma (sop.) | VIC red seals in 74000-88000 zone may be worth $3-6. |
| GORITZ, Otto (bar.) | 64000, 74000 VIC red seals (1911-13): $3-5. |
| GRANFORTE, Apollo (bar.) | 1925 VIC red seals 1114, 6541, 6542: $3-5. |
| GRAYVILL, Jose (sop.) | COL sides in 3000, A 5000, C 1000 series (1907-08): $5-9. |

# H

| | |
|---|---|
| HACKETT, Charles (ten.) | Some COL discs in the 9000M series (1919-25): $3-6. |
| HAMLIN, George (ten.) | VIC red seals in 64000, 74000 series (1908-15): $3-5. |
| HARROLD, Orville (ten.) | COL sides in A 2000, A 5400, A 5800 series: $3-5. |
| HEMPEL, Frieda (sop.) | $3-7 for VIC red seals in 87000-89000 sequences (1912-17). |
| HOMER, Louise (cont.) | Generally $3-5. Some VIC red seals in 85000, 89000 blocs may be valued as high as $12. |

# I

| | |
|---|---|
| IVOGUN, Maria (sop.) | BRN sides (1923-25) in 10000, 15000, 30000, 50000 series fall into $3-6 range. |

# J

| | |
|---|---|
| JADLOWKER, Herman (ten.) | VIC red seals $5-7 in 76000, 88000-89000 series. |

| | |
|---|---|
| JEFFERSON, Joseph (actor) | COL discs (1903) 1468-69, A 395, 390: $10-20. |
| JERITZA, Maria (sop.) | VIC red seals in 1000, 6100, 6300, 6500 series $3-6. |
| JOURNET, Marcel (bass) | 1905 COL recordings in 3100 series $3-5. Red seal VICs in 81000-89000 series, 6100-8000 series also, $4-8. |
| JUCH, Emma (sop.) | 1904 VIC red seals in 64000, 74000, 81000, 85000 series: $6-10. |

## K

| | |
|---|---|
| KING, Roxy (sop.) | 1908-09 red seals VIC discs (64000, 74000) about $3-5. |
| KIRKBY-LUNN, Louise (cont.) | COL records from 1905 (3278, 3279): $7. |
| KOSHETZ, Nina (sop.) | 1922-23 BRN sides in 10000, 15000, 30000, 50000 series $3-5. |
| KRISTMANN, Emilia (sop.) | Red seal VIC sides (1903) in 5000, 91000 series: $3-6. |
| KRUSZELNICKA, Salomea (sop.) | VIC red seal 61078 (1903): $4. |
| KURT, Melanie (sop.) | COL sides (1917) E 3274, E 5139 perhaps $5-7. |

## L

| | |
|---|---|
| LAMONT, Forrest (ten.) | 1919-20 OKE discs in 6000 series: $3-5. |
| LAURI-VOLPI, Giacomo (ten.) | $4-7 for some of his BRN sides in 15000, 5000 series. |
| LAZARO, Hipolito (ten.) | COL sides in 7000-8900 ''M'' series about $4-6. |

LAZZARI, Virgilio (bass)

1922-24 VOC discs in 30000, 52000 series $3-5.

LIPKOWSKA, Lydia (sop.)

COL sides (ca. 1911) in 30000, A 5200 series $4-8.

LITVINNE, Felia (sop.)

VIC red seal 5111 (1903) at about $10. VIC 91052: $5.

# M

MAETERLINCK, Georgette (sop.)

COL discs (1912-13) A 1153, A 1243 perhaps $5.

MARCEL, Lucille (sop.)

VIC 76018 ($4), COL A5482 (1913) about $5.

MARCONI, Francesco (ten.)

VIC red seals 76004, 88226, 89046: $4-6.

MARDONES, Jose (bass)

COL discs (1910-23) in the "A", "M" series may be worth $3-6; VIC 6000's perhaps $6.

MARSH, Lucy (sop.)

VIC 8034 with John McCormack (1913-14) at $7.

MARTIN, Riccardo (ten.)

Red seal VIC sides (1910-11) in 87000-88000 series: $5-7.

| | |
|---|---|
| MARTINELLI, Giovanni (ten.) | VIC red seals in 700, 6100 blocs $4-6 (1914-18). |
| MATZENAUER, Margarete (cont.) | VIC red seal in 87000-89000 zones $3-7. COL discs (1915) in A 5600 series: $4. Same for later VICs in 6000 sequence. |
| MC CORMACK, John (ten.) | Very little above $3 for his many VIC sides (1910-25). |
| MELBA, Nellie (sop.) | VIC mauve label (1904-05) sides in 94000-95000 series $5-7. Red seals in 88000, 89000 blocs $3-8. |
| METZGER, Ottilie (cont.) | COL A5565 (1914) in vicinity of $8. |
| MIURA, Tamaki (sop.) | COL 49260, 49265 (1917) perhaps $3-4. |

## N

| | |
|---|---|
| NIELSEN, Alice (sop.) | VIC red seals in 64000, 74000 (1907-08) $3-7. COL discs in A 5000's: $3-6. |
| NORDICA, Lillian (sop.) | COL discs (1907-11) in 30000, 68000D series perhaps $6-10. |
| NOTE, Jean (bar.) | 1903 VIC red seals 5074, 5084 about $8. |
| NUIBO, Francisco (ten.) | Red seal VIC sides (1905) in 81000, 85000 series $3-5. COL discs in 3100 bloc $3-4. |

## O

| | |
|---|---|
| OBER, Margarete (cont.) | VIC red seals (1914-17) in 64000, 74000 sequences: $4-7. |
| OLITZKA, Rosa (cont.) | COL sides in A 1300, A 5300 series (1912-13) $10. |

ONEGIN, Sigrid (cont.)

BRN sides (1922-25) in 10000, 15000, 50000 series: $3-7.

# P

PADEREWSKI, Ignace (piano)

Most under $3, except for 6000 series: $3-4.

PALET, Jose (ten.)

VIC red seals in 6300 sequence (1920-23) perhaps close to $3-5.

PAOLI, Antonio (ten.)

VIC red seals 1908-10 in the 88000-92000 series: $3-6.

PATTI, Adelina (sop.)

VIC red seal Patti sides (1906) in 95000 series: $5-7.

PIETRACEWSKA, Carolina (cont.)

1910-11 VIC red seal sides 88225, 88269: $4-5.

PINZA, Ezio (bass)

Early (1925) VIC red seal sides in 1100, 6500 groupings: $4-5.

PLANCON, Pol (bass)

1903 VIC red seals in 5000 series $12-17. Average for discs in 81000-95000 sequences drops off to $4-8.

PONSELLE, Rosa (sop.)

COL discs with "D", "M" suffixes: $3-6. VIC red seals in 6400 series, $7 on the whole.

# R

RACHMANINOFF, Sergei (piano)

Very seldom over $3. A few 6000 series at $4.

RAISA, Rosa (sop.)

VOC sides of the early 1920s in the 30000, 52000, 60000, and 70000 series: $3-7.

REISS, Albert (ten.)

VIC red seals (64000, 74000) from 1911 about $4-6.

RENAUD, Maurice (bar.)

Early (1903) red seal VIC records in 5000 block: $9-12. Down to

| | $4-7 for VIC discs in 91000-92000 series. |
| --- | --- |
| RETHBERG, Elisabeth (sop.) | BRN sides in the 10000, 15000, 50000 sequences: $3-7. |
| RIMINI, Giacomo (bar.) | For 1923-24 VOC sides (60000, 70000 series) about $3-5. |
| ROTHIER, Leon (bass) | 1916-18 COL sides in A 5800, A 5900 series $4-5. |
| RUFFO, Titta (bar.) | A few VIC red seals in 1000, 6000, 8000 groupings $4-7. |
| RUSZCOWSKA, Elena (sop.) | A modest $3-5 for her 1902-12 VIC red seals in 88000-89000, and 8000 series. |

## S

| | |
| --- | --- |
| SAMMARCO, Mario (bar.) | $4-9 for his 1910-11 VIC red seals in 87000-89000 series. |
| SCHIPA, Tito (ten.) | VIC red seals scattered through 800, 900, 1000, 6000 series: $3-5. |
| SCHORR, Friedrich (bar.) | 1924-25 BRN sides in 10000, 15000 series: $3-4. |
| SCHUMANN-HEINK, Ernestine (cont.) | Early (1903) COL sides (1378-82): $30. Most of her VIC red seals $3-5, with a few exceptions at $4-6 in the 6000 series. |
| SCOTNEY, Evelyn (sop.) | VOC sides (1920-24) in 70000 bloc may reach $4-5. |
| SCOTTI, Antonio (bar.) | 1903 COL sides (1205-1207, A 620) at about $30. Some VIC red seals (85000 series) may reach $8-9. |
| SEMBACH, Johannes (ten.) | COL sides (1916-17) in the A 5800, E 3000, E 5000 series $4-6. |

| | |
|---|---|
| SEMBRICH, Marcella (sop.) | Uncommon 1903 COL sides (1364-66, or, A 618) at $30. VIC red seals in 81000-95000 blocs: $3-10. |
| SISTINE CHAPEL (choir) | Early (1903) VIC red seals 5064-67: $3-5. |
| SLEZAK, Leo (ten.) | VIC red seals in 61000-74000 series (1909-10): $3-5. COL sides A 5385-96 higher at about $7. |
| SMIRNOV, Dmitri (ten.) | VIC red seals (1922-23) in 66000, 74000 series $3-5. |
| SORO, Cristina (sop.) | 64000-74000 series VIC red seals (1918-23): $3-5. |
| SPENCER, Janet (cont.) | VIC red seals (64000-74000) about $3-7. |
| STRACCIARI, Riccardo (bar.) | COL discs in "D", "M" series (1917-25): $3-5. |
| SUNDELIUS, Marie (sop.) | 1920-22 VOC sides in 30000, 52000, 60000, 70000 series: $3-6. |
| SWARTZ, Jeska (mez.-sop.) | COL record A 5438 (1913): $4. |

# T

| | |
|---|---|
| TAMAGNO, Francesco (ten.) | 1904 VIC red seals in 95000 bloc: $5. |
| TETRAZZINI, Luisa (sop.) | Rare ZON sides in 2500, 10000 series (1903): $10-12. Later VIC red seals (8800-92000) $3-7. |
| TEYTE, Maggie (sop.) | COL sides from 1914-16 in "A" series: $3-4. |
| TOKATYAN, Armand (ten.) | VOC sides from mid-twenties in 55000, 60000, 7000 series: $3-5. |
| TRENTINI, Emma (sop.) | 1907-08 COL sides (30087, 30122, A 5026): $5-7. |

# V

VAN HOOSE, Ellison (ten.)     VIC red seals in 74000-95000 series: $4-6. COL A 5352: $4.

VAN ROOY, Anton (bar.)     1906-09 COL sides in 30000 bloc (and A 5000 series): $7-12. VIC 92062: $5.

# W

WHITE, Carolina (sop.)     COL sides in 30000, 36000 (plus "A" suffixes): $3-7.

WITHERSPOON, Herbert (bass)  VIC red seals in 74000 bloc: $3-6.

WRIGHT, Rosa (cont.)     1906 COL sides 3502, 30031: $3-4.

# Y

YAW, Ellen (sop.)     1907 VIC red seals 64000, 74000 series: $5-7.

242

# Z

| | |
|---|---|
| ZENATELLO, Giovanni (ten.) | COL discs in 30000, 36000, "A" series: $4-8. |
| ZEPPILLI, Alice (sop.) | COL disc from 1912, A 1213: $4. |
| ZEROLA, Nicola (ten.) | VIC red seals in 45000-88000 blocs (1912-24): $3-6. |

*Footnote to Readers:* I feel compelled to remind you that the prices suggested relate to the garden variety classical 78 rpms many Americans have "around the house," as it were. You should be aware that for some records made by these very same artists much higher prices are asked and are paid. Should you have records made for labels such as HMV, Pathé Actuelle, Gramophone, Odeon, Parlophone, and Fonotipia you may assume, in general, that several more dollars may be added to these essentially domestic prices. Remember also that the prices quoted are predicated on the assumption that the records are in excellent condition. Also keep your eyes open for infrequent but informative articles on the classical market, such as Carol Poston's, "Jazz, Opera, 'Entertainers' Put Gold in Old Records," *American Collector* (June, 1979), pp. 4-5, 24, 27. As always, if there is the slightest question in your mind as to the value of a given record, retain it until you have investigated further.

# L'Envoi

By way of tidying up, I ought to bring some specificity to items mentioned in passing in the text of this *Guide*. For example, you may feel the need to contact a number of *professional dealers* for purposes of purchasing or selling 78 rpm discs. If so, I recommend you consult the following sources. Prices of these outlets are subject to change, of course. Lists of dealers may be found in:

Randall C. Hill, *Collectible Rock Records* (House of Collectibles, Orlando, Florida, 1979), pp. 355-391. Price: $8.95.

Jerry Osborne, *Popular and Rock Records: 1948-1978* (O'Sullivan, Woodside and Company, Phoenix, Arizona, 1978), pp. 237-251. Price: $7.95.

*Kastlemusick Monthly Bulletin* and the annual, two-volume *Kastlemusick Directory for Collectors*. Both are published in Wilmington, Delaware, at 901 Washington Street, zip code 19801. A subscription to the *Bulletin* is $9.84 a year. The *Directory* is $12.95 for both volumes.

*The Record Finder*, published at 15934 Warwick Boulevard, Newport News, Virginia 23602. Ten issues per year for $6. Devoted primarily to sales lists but includes a classified page on which dealers are often listed.

Although I have no vested interest in their businesses, I do want to mention a few dealerships with whom I have enjoyed a satisfying personal and professional relationship in recent years. Perhaps you would wish to establish contact with them and engage in dialogue about the popular and/or classical 78 rpm market:

Bob Andrews Records. P.O. Box 7000-115, Redondo Beach, CA 90277.

Don and Lou Donahue. Write to them in care of The Olde Tyme Music Scene, 915 Main Street, Boonton, NJ 07205.

Leon Kloppholz ("Mr. Records") at P.O. Box 764, Hillside, NJ 07205.

John C. Sicignano. Located at 29 Columbia Avenue, Nutley, NJ 07110.

As you investigate these available sources you will find that they lead you to others. These recommendations are offered as ignitions and are by no means exhaustive. I merely wish to help you take the first step on the intriguing journey through the labyrinth of record dealing and collecting. Now you are on your own. Good luck and good listening.

# INDEX

TODD, Dick, 197
TRACE, Al, 197
TROTTER, John Scott, 197
TROUBADOURS, 197
TRUMBAUER, Frankie, 197
TUCKER, Orrin, 200
TUCKER, Sophie, 200
TUCKER, Tommy, 200
TUCKER ORCH., 200

UNIVERSITY ORCH., 200

VALLEE, Rudy, 200, 202
VENUTI, Joe, 202
VORHEES, Don, 202

WALD, Jerry, 202
WALDORF ASTORIA ORCH., 202
WALLER, Fats, 202-203
WARING, Fred, 203
WARNOW, Mark, 203
WEBB, Chick, 203
WEBER, Marek, 203
WEEKS, Anson, 208
WEEMS, Ted, 208
WELK, Lawrence, 208
WHITE, Lew, 208
WHITEMAN, Paul, 208, 211
WHITING, Margaret, 211
WILLIAMS, Bert, 211
WILLIAMS, Clarence, 211-213
WILLIAMS, Griff, 213
WILLSON, Meredith, 213
WILSON, Teddy, 213, 215

YERKES, Harry, 215
YOUNG, Victor, 215

ZOLLO, Leo, 215
ZURKE, Bob, 215

## CLASSICAL ARTISTS

ABOTT, Bessie, 223
ACKTE, Aino, 223
ADAMS, Suzanne, 223
AFFRE, Augustarello, 223
AGUSSOL, Charlotte, 223
ALBANI, Carlo, 223
ALDA, Frances, 223
ALTHOUSE, Paul, 223
AMATO, Pasquale, 223
ANCONA, Mario, 223
ANSSEAU, Fernand, 223
ARIMONDI, Vittorio, 223
ARRAL, Blanche, 224
AUSTRAL, Florence, 224

BAKLANOFF, George, 224
BARRIENTOS, Maria, 224
BATTISTINI, Mattia, 224
BEDDOE, Daniel, 224
BELLATTI, Virgilio, 224
BERTANA, Luisa, 224
BESANZONI, Gabriella, 224
BISPHAM, David, 225
BLANCHART, Ramon, 225
BLASS, Robert, 225
BLAUVELT, Lillian, 225
BOHNEN, Michael, 225
BONCI, Alessandro, 225
BONINSEGNA, Celestina, 225
BORI, Lucrezia, 225
BORONAT, Olimpia, 225
BRASLAU, Sophie, 225
BRONSKAJA, Eugenie, 225

253

# *About the Author*

To quote Soderbergh on Soderbergh, "I am neither a professional dealer nor a compulsive collector of 78's. I do have a modest cache of records from the period 1920-1957 but they are dear friends, not marketable properties. Simply speaking, I am a private citizen who has rummaged around in the facts, folklore, and fun of old records."

In addition, Brooklyn-born Peter Soderbergh, Ph.D, is the Dean of the College of Education, Louisiana State University; the author of this book and *78 rpm Records & Prices* (both published by Wallace-Homestead Book Co.); plus over sixty articles on a variety of topics such as cinema, children's literature, education, United States social and intellectual history, and several biographies. Soderbergh is listed in *Who's Who: Leaders in Education* and is currently writing a history of Special Education in the United States which will be published in 1981.